TALES OF TERROR'S
DECADES OF TERROR 2019
1990'S SLASHER FILMS

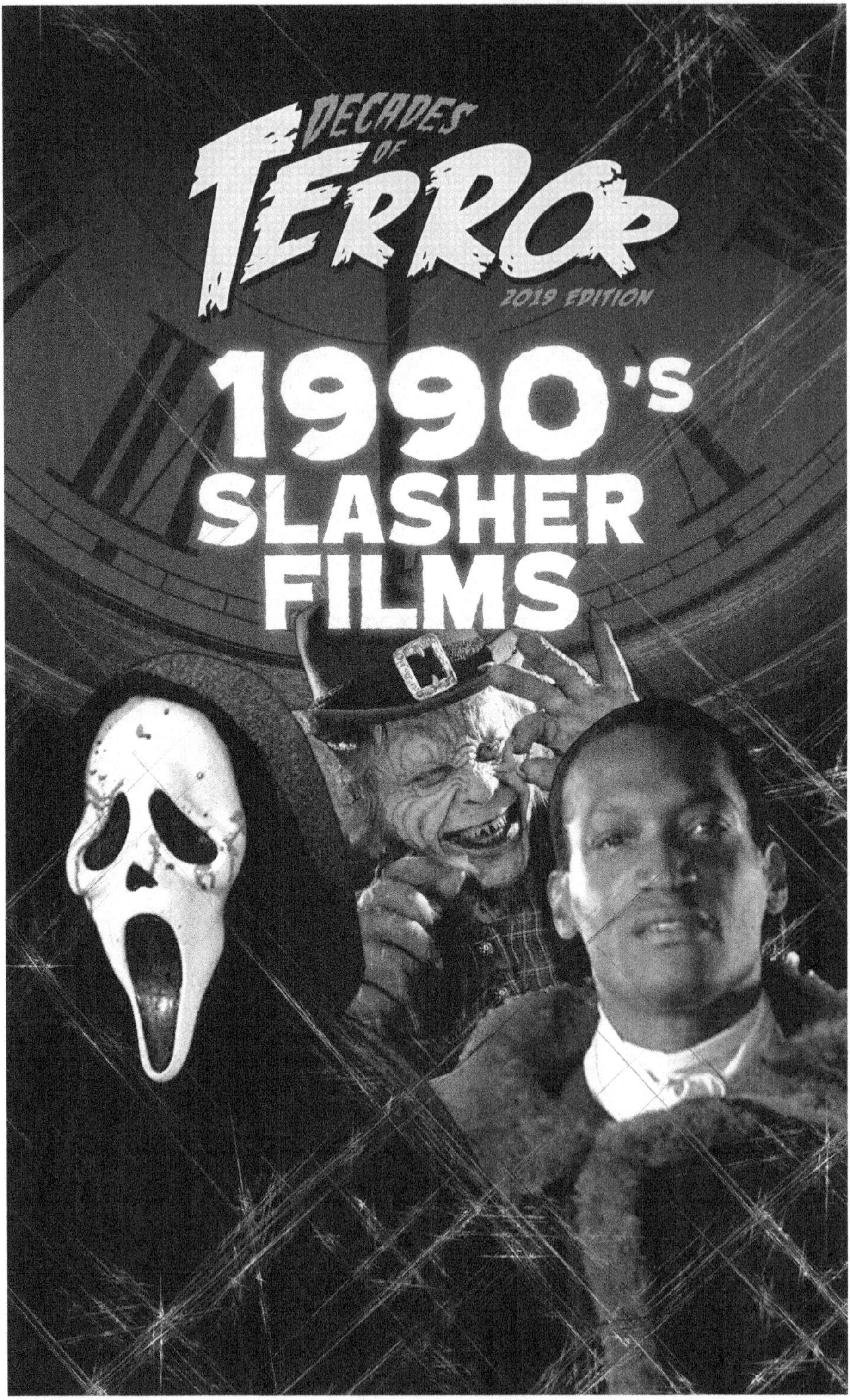

DECADES OF TERROR
2019 EDITION

1990'S SLASHER FILMS

FEATURING

STEVE HUTCHISON
CRITIC

Copyright © 2019 by Steve Hutchison
All rights reserved. This book or any portion thereof may not be reproduced or used in any manner whatsoever without the express written permission of the publisher except for the use of brief quotations in a book review or scholarly journal.

First Printing: 2019
ISBN-13: 978-1074050481

Bookstores and wholesalers: Please contact books@terror.ca.

Tales of Terror
tales@terror.ca
www.terror.ca

INTRODUCTION

Steve Hutchison reviews 100 amazing slasher films from the 1990's. Each film is analyzed and discussed with a synopsis and a rating. The movies are ranked from best to worst. How many have you seen?

CONTENTS

- 7 INTRODUCTION
- 14 SCREAM
- 15 CHILD'S PLAY 2
- 16 THE FACULTY
- 17 ARACHNOPHOBIA
- 18 FREDDY'S DEAD: THE FINAL NIGHTMARE
- 19 NIGHT OF THE DEMONS 2
- 20 TREMORS
- 21 THE FRIGHTENERS
- 22 HOUSE ON HAUNTED HILL
- 23 SPECIES
- 24 NEW NIGHTMARE
- 25 SCREAM 2
- 26 CANDYMAN
- 27 CUBE
- 28 DEEP BLUE SEA
- 29 SLEEPY HOLLOW
- 30 CHILD'S PLAY 3
- 31 FRANKENHOOKER
- 32 HELLRAISER: BLOODLINE
- 33 POPCORN
- 34 DR. GIGGLES
- 35 HALLOWEEN H20: 20 YEARS LATER

36	HELLRAISER III: HELL ON EARTH
37	DISTURBING BEHAVIOR
38	PET SEMATARY II
39	BRIDE OF CHUCKY
40	IDLE HANDS
41	FROM DUSK TILL DAWN 2: TEXAS BLOOD MONEY
42	KOLOBOS
43	PREDATOR 2
44	PSYCHO
45	SLEEPWALKERS
46	I KNOW WHAT YOU DID LAST SUMMER
47	GRAVEYARD SHIFT
48	ALIEN: RESURRECTION
49	PUPPET MASTER II
50	PROM NIGHT III: THE LAST KISS
51	LEPRECHAUN 3
52	PUPPET MASTER III: TOULON'S REVENGE
53	WISHMASTER
54	WISHMASTER 2: EVIL NEVER DIES
55	CHILDREN OF THE CORN III: URBAN HARVEST
56	NIGHT OF THE DEMONS III
57	URBAN LEGEND
58	JASON GOES TO HELL: THE FINAL FRIDAY
59	THE LAWNMOWER MAN

60	*I STILL KNOW WHAT YOU DID LAST SUMMER*
61	*THE DENTIST*
62	*PSYCHO IV: THE BEGINNING*
63	*THE DARK HALF*
64	*ALIEN³*
65	*SPECIES II*
66	*FROM DUSK TILL DAWN 3: THE HANGMAN'S DAUGHTER*
67	*LEPRECHAUN*
68	*PUMPKINHEAD II: BLOOD WINGS*
69	*MOSQUITO*
70	*MANIAC COP 3: BADGE OF SILENCE*
71	*PINOCCHIO'S REVENGE*
72	*UNCLE SAM*
73	*WARLOCK: THE ARMAGEDDON*
74	*SOMETIMES THEY COME BACK... AGAIN*
75	*SOMETIMES THEY COME BACK*
76	*SCANNERS III: THE TAKEOVER*
77	*CASTLE FREAK*
78	*MIKEY*
79	*KILLER TONGUE*
80	*DEMONIC TOYS*
81	*SILENT NIGHT, DEADLY NIGHT 5: THE TOY MAKER*
82	*CANDYMAN: FAREWELL TO THE FLESH*
83	*DOLLY DEAREST*

84	LEPRECHAUN 2
85	CANDYMAN: DAY OF THE DEAD
86	976-EVIL II
87	GHOULIES III: GHOULIES GO TO COLLEGE
88	HALLOWEEN: THE CURSE OF MICHAEL MYERS
89	PIRANHA
90	THE DENTIST 2
91	SLUMBER PARTY MASSACRE III
92	SORORITY HOUSE MASSACRE II
93	THE UNNAMABLE II: THE STATEMENT OF RANDOLPH CARTER
94	MANIAC COP 2
95	TREMORS II: AFTERSHOCKS
96	JACK FROST
97	OMEN IV: THE AWAKENING
98	PSYCHO COP RETURNS
99	OFFICE KILLER
100	FUNNY MAN
101	CRITTERS 3
102	HARD TO DIE
103	PROM NIGHT IV: DELIVER US FROM EVIL
104	CRITTERS 4
105	LEPRECHAUN 4: IN SPACE
106	CHILDREN OF THE CORN V: FIELDS OF TERROR
107	SILENT PREDATORS

108	NIGHT OF THE DRIBBLER
109	STEPFATHER III
110	BAD CHANNELS
111	CURSE OF THE PUPPET MASTER
112	TROLL 2
113	TERROR FIRMER

SCREAM

1996

High schoolers recognize horror movie patterns in the recent deaths of other students.

Slashers were among the most successful subgenres of horror in the 70's and 80's, and then they became predictable, tired, soon before they completely ran out of momentum in the early 90's. Scream reboots the trend by now fleshing out characters that live in the same world horror movie fans do, with Freddy Krueger, Jason Voorhees, Michael Myers and other horror villains constantly referenced.

This is both a slasher and a whodunit, but it features protagonists who try to overcome a series of murders by what they ironically have in common, as friends: their knowledge and love of horror movies. The actors are a well assorted and written bunch that does an impeccable job of reminiscing the subgenre while juggling with a complex underlying mystery the movie heavily relies on.

The jump scares are deserved; written and directed with ideal pacing, dialog, acting and a production value rarely matched by similar movies. The intricate script throws you in all directions, and stays away from the red stuff as much as it can. Scream stimulates you mentally, proving that a good movie, disregarding its classification, can only spawn from a good story.

8/8

CHILD'S PLAY 2

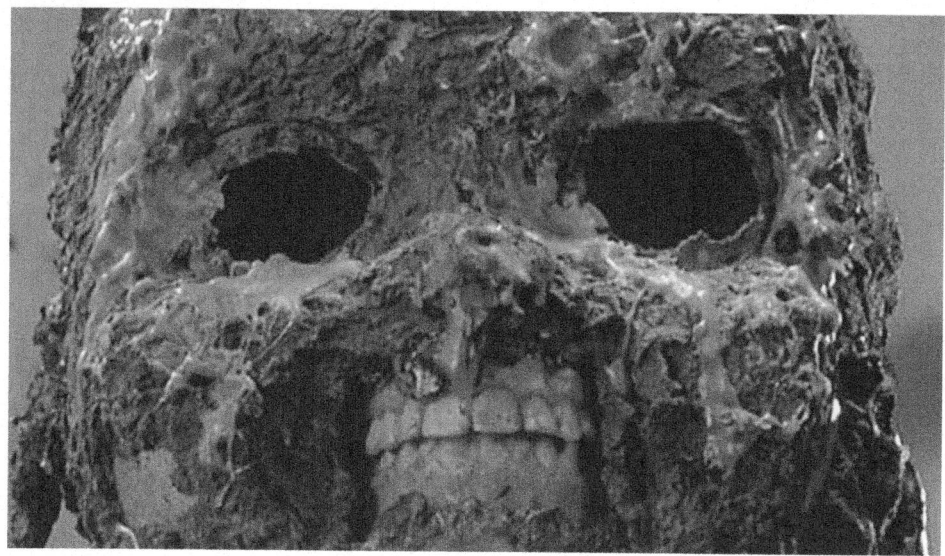

1990

An adopted boy once the victim of a possessed doll suspects it found its way to his new foster home.

Chucky's no longer an enigma. We've seen him walk, talk and stalk already and this means we now get more explicit exposure, fewer chills, but more amusing murders and one-liners. The doll is scary enough on its own but it can no longer rely on our apprehension and imagination. Fortunately, the script avoids most pitfalls of horror sequels.

Two of our three main protagonists from the original are not returning and the story centers on Andy, the kid, instead. Considering he is who Chucky's after, this isn't much of an issue. Child's Play 2 goes all out when it comes to special effects and uses no shortcut to impress us. Most of them are rendered through puppet work and animatronics, with the occasional midget thrown in the mix.

This holds up to the original in terms of writing, directing and acting but it has more ambition. It is arguably a perfect sequel. It brings back most of the elements that worked the first time but the script has fun with them and pushes the concept to the extreme. This is a more prestigious movie than its predecessor was, with a grand finale you will not easily forget.

8/8

THE FACULTY

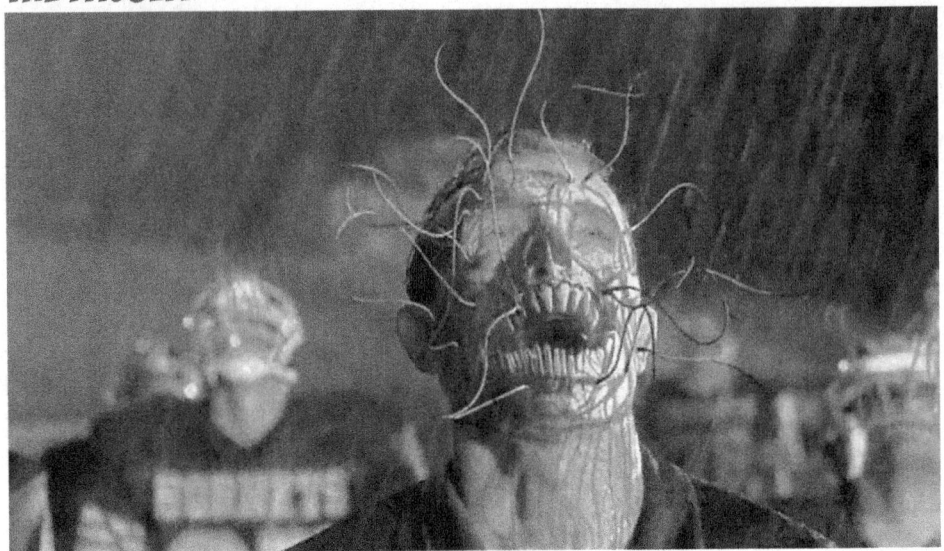

1998

Six students find out their teachers are from another planet.

A splendid cast is introduced very early on, including the protagonists who are presented through character cards right after an epic prologue. There are obvious Body Snatchers and Scream influences, here. It's no coincidence that Kevin Williamson, of Scream fame, is screenwriting. The Faculty is punctuated by an amazing rock soundtrack just when you think the film couldn't get any cooler.

The students, in The Faculty, are mentally and physically abusive, from the get go, so we're not sure exactly what they become when they're "possessed", and that's a grey zone that never gets addressed. Some of the "infected" become more aggressive and some more passive. All characters are right out of a comic book and the acting is irreproachable. In fact, the film itself is almost perfect.

The Faculty is as mainstream as horror films get, but horror buffs will see it from a particular angle. It's an alien invasion, a slasher, a whodunit and, well, it's teen horror. What else is there to like? The actors are amazing: Josh Hartnett, Famke Janssen, Robert Patrick, Laura Harris, Salma Hayek, Piper Laurie, Usher Raymond and Elijah Wood, to name a few.

8/8

ARACHNOPHOBIA

1990

A species of killer spiders starts to breed and kill.

"Arachnophobia" refers to Jeff Daniel's character's uncontrollable fear of spiders. For a good while, people around him die mysteriously and he gets blamed for it, as their doctor. The inhabitants of the town he just moved in don't see what we see. We witness it all. The camera constantly impersonates a breed of killer spiders we know just got imported mistakenly. We see them kill.

The way the camera treats the victims and the spiders is reminiscent of slasher flicks of the preceding decade. But, that's not all Arachnophobia is. The film isn't supernatural, but it's not exactly probable or even plausible. It's a thriller with solid jump scares and the kind of suspense the 1990's are known for. It's not a comedy but it's funny when it chooses to be.

To have various spiders follow established trajectories and interact with actors, all with perfect timing, is pure genius. The movie constantly impresses by the way it presents the spider. This subgenre is rarely taken seriously. There is no CG, here. What you see is what you get. The acting is impeccable. The casting is more than you can ask for. This is horror filmmaking at its best.

8/8

FREDDY'S DEAD: THE FINAL NIGHTMARE

1991

An amnesic teenager who fears sleep is brought to a shelter and is evaluated by mystified specialists.

The sixth Nightmare on Elm Street movie deals with the little damage left to be done in Springwood. Freddy's goal was to wipe out the whole teenage population in town and he's almost there. This is the apocalyptic one. The script is evidently setup so to feel like it truly is the end, and while no character is ever joyful, here, Freddy compensates with a humor more witty and eccentric than ever.

The murder scenes are their imaginative self, but they are more slapstick, emotionless. Freddy's world is now that of a cartoon, or a video game, and is still so very iconic, so atmospheric, that the film manages to be both creepy and mesmerizing at once. Well-orchestrated photography highly contributes to this, as reality blends with dream and set designs gradually distort into an astral prison.

Freddy's Dead is the best looking film in the Nightmare on Elm Street franchise, but not the most organic. It's a sequel that comes full circle, referencing the past, reinterpreting scenes from its own franchise, and partially acting as prequel; all this cleverly narrated through a procedural, flashbacks and psychic dreams.

NIGHT OF THE DEMONS 2

1994

Teenagers unknowingly carry a demon curse from a haunted house to their school on Halloween night.

1988's Night of the Demons was self-contained. Against all odds, Joe Augustyn performs a tour de force, here; powerful enough to bring back all the elements that made the original a classic, and carries the action from the haunted house to a Catholic boarding school; the second next best context for sexually frustrated teenagers. This is pretext, of course, for brattiness and blood...

The only thing the original had that the sequel doesn't is script purity. The arc was simple, and so were the characters. The writing is more layered in Part 2 and not as lively, but continuity is ensured by creative minds. As a sequel, it succeeds in further exposing the virulence of its creature with little redundancy: they are re-established as sexual demons that rely on fluids to possess.

Aside from centering on religion and the occult, the film meets every standard set by the original: deliberately bad but not terrible actors, imaginative practical effects, shock value, teen hormones and a lot of partying. Night of the Demons 2, like its predecessor, is more entertaining than intellectual, more humorous than dramatic, but manages to mix comedy and horror in 80's retro fashion.

7/8

TREMORS

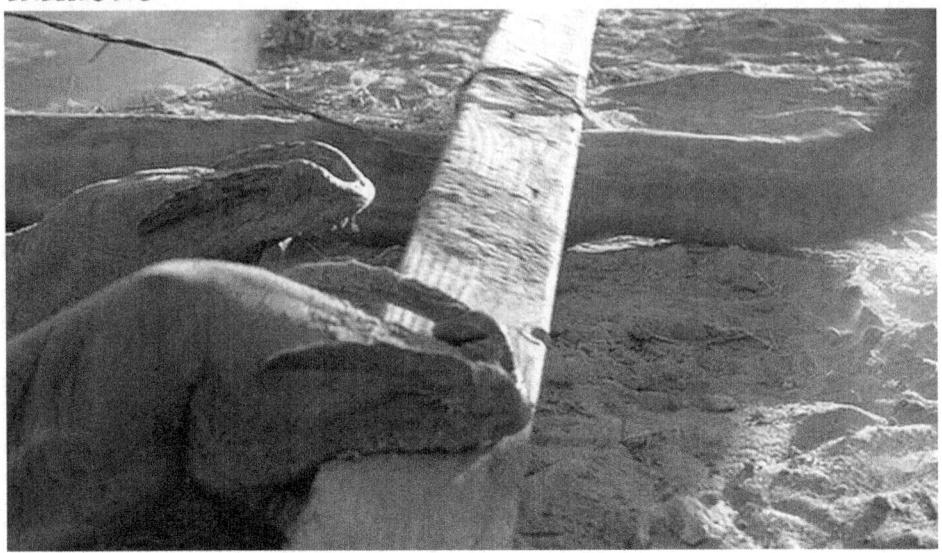

1990

The inhabitants of a desert town are attacked by prehistoric worms sensitive to vibrations.

Kevin Bacon's character is a simple man with nothing better to do than to kill giant worms. He is the reason this horror movie is funny without resorting to slapstick comedy. The main protagonists are depicted as tough, manly, simple and unimpressionable. They don't care how big their problem is; they just want it fixed. They aren't your vulnerable whiners. What's more, they have an arsenal...

1990's Tremors features creatures unlike anything we've seen before. They live underground, are good crawlers, vicious killers and detect human vibrations. The script makes good use of this gimmick and creates a fake context and fake conditions to instigate a fear that the viewer never experienced; in life or on film: for most of the runtime, the protagonists must avoid stepping on the ground...

They jump from rock to boulder and climb buildings to avoid being eaten by truly frightening monsters. The support cast is there to be dispatched, to ensure balanced gore and to reinforce the slasher vibe while Bacon makes us feel secure and tries to figure the whole thing out. Tremors could've been the worst b-schlock to ever surface; instead it is a brilliant hybrid of dark subgenres.

THE FRIGHTENERS

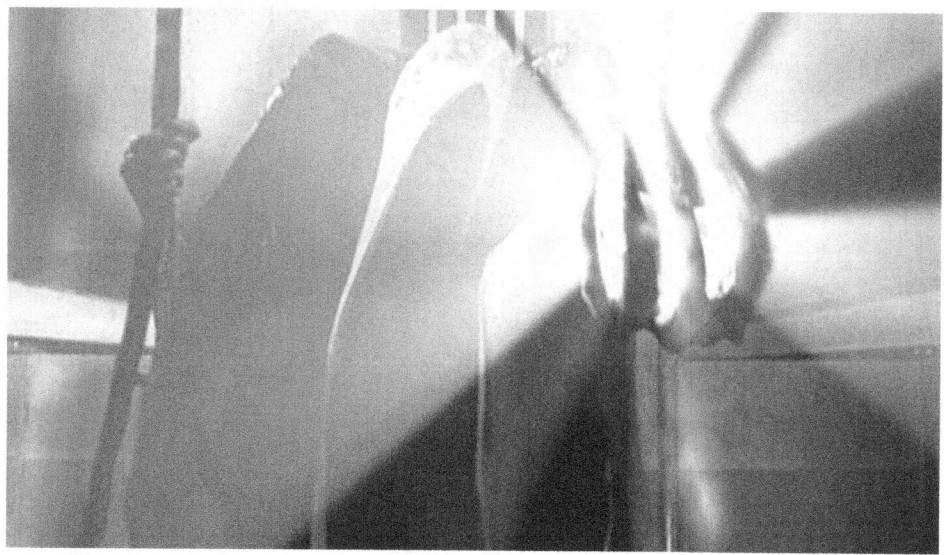

1996

A man who can communicate with the dead has to stop a demonic entity from killing people.

The planets aligned when Peter Jackson shot The Frighteners. The film contains more special effects than the average production of its time. Despite the intensive computer-generated imagery, the visuals look amazing. Jackson is aiming for a cartoonish look more than realism. The photography and the editing are impeccable but there are too many flashbacks. Danny Elfman's handling the score.

The actors are equally astonishing. Michael J. Fox is the ultimate American protagonist. He's likable and sympathetic. His character has brilliant chemistry with ghosts. Trini Alvarado is his love interest and we instantly appreciate her presence. Jeffrey Combs, known for complex roles in classic horror movies, plays one of the most eccentric characters of his career and that means a lot!

There is an equal dose of drama and comedy. We often go from sadness and sorrow to slapstick humor in a matter of seconds, and it doesn't feel awkward. There's virtually nothing wrong with this movie. What's more, The Frighteners features one of the coolest villains ever depicted in horror movies, a mix between a reaper and a ghost. It looks cool as hell!

7/8

HOUSE ON HAUNTED HILL

1999

Six strangers are invited by a rich couple to spend the night in a supposedly haunted asylum in exchange for a million dollars.

House on Haunted Hill is the remake of a horror movie by the same title released 40 years earlier. It is an upgrade on every level. The budget, the performances, the special effects and the set design; the production as a whole meets Hollywood standards. The story is structured like the original, but with greatly augmented humor, attitude, gore and scares.

The "house" is an old asylum rigged to lock its occupants in, which occurs sooner than later. It is undoubtedly one of the creepiest in horror history. It keeps us guessing whether this is all a game or if the ghosts of dead patients are more than a legend. The clever whodunit tangent adds to the initial mystery; a fascinating note played by the film for a long time.

House on Haunted Hill carries the burden of a major flaw, but it is limited to a few scenes: although the compositing is highly effective, the 3-D effects are far from photorealistic. There is compensation, though. Character exposition and their cohesion work admirably. The script is smart, evenly paced, dense, but not overly, and will have you on the edge of your seat from beginning to end.

7/8

SPECIES

1995

An alien hybrid escaped from a laboratory is hunted down by a team of specialists.

The quintessential horror movie villain is historically male and the main victim female. The roles are switched, here, in a sensual, sexy and sexual high-end supernatural thriller with gore and strong elements of science-fiction and action. The main protagonist, a femme fatale and the ultimate threat, uses seduction as a weapon and a means to an end: she needs human sperm to reproduce.

The actors are all excellent. They are perfectly in tone with a screenplay that only moves forward and fast. Like the good guys, we're always two steps behind the monster, though we see her murdering people and getting naked. Natasha Henstridge is beautiful and can act. She makes us believe one can murder innocently. She delivers a sometimes titillating, sometimes unnerving performance.

Because this is a slasher, the writer depicted her as some kind of black widow or succubus. She picks her men carefully, avoiding weak genes and disease when she detects it. She is a metaphor to romantic fears some have. It took a 1990's melodramatic thriller to address the subject, something few films have before. The end result is a relatable, tense and scary ride with clever twists and turns.

7/8

NEW NIGHTMARE

1994

Filmmakers rebooting a popular horror franchise find themselves endangered by a real-life manifestation of the antagonist featured in the script.

Wes Craven's self-referential sequel, technically a spin-off of A Nightmare on Elm Street but part of the collection, tells the hypothetical story of the artists, cast and crew, responsible for the success of the franchise discovering they are being haunted by the creature they gave life to, as if subject to a pop culture egregore.

The great script, cinematography and performances, including a plausible child actor that isn't annoying, make New Nightmare stand out in the series. It is down to earth and watered down in terms of scares, surrealism and gore, and no longer fun, let alone funny. The original film worked on an emotional level more than its sequels did because it took this path. Like this one, it was much sinister.

A lot of familiar names, actors from previous films, namely, play themselves. Some are mere cameos; others have a significance in the plot. Clues, winks and homages are there to be found by the true fan. In this, Heather Langenkamp, the "Nancy" character, has a child of her own and lives with the fear she helped spread on screen: the fear that sleep is coming to get you and the ones you love.

7/8

SCREAM 2

1997

A teenager whose friends were murdered by obsessed horror movie fans suspects she is now being stalked by a copycat.

The original Scream remodeled the slasher trend by thinking outside the box and surprising the tired fan with its intricate structure, it's self-referencing patterns and its legendary twist. Does Scream 2 live up to expectations? Mostly. We resume our story with the surviving cast members that now carry the weight of the first film on their shoulders and don't exactly feel like partying, anymore.

Support actors take care of ensuring the fun vibe. The returning characters are slightly older and they moved on with their lives, only to be reunited again in a different setting. This time, the action mostly takes place in a world of fraternities, sororities, keggers and togas. It's still a whodunit slasher that references its own subgenre. Additionally, it now plays on the tropes of sequels.

Not as clean and simple, and not as bubbly as its predecessor but very entertaining, nonetheless, Scream 2 has the same "meta" approach Scream had, in that it speaks to the audience without breaking the 4th wall. Brilliantly written and directed, it is among the most high-end slasher films. It shows virtually no flaw, aside from having to live up to a golden classic.

7/8

CANDYMAN

1992

A university student writing her thesis on local urban legends meddles with a dangerous ghost.

Candyman, like Nightmare on Elm Street and Hellraiser, is a borderline slasher begging for a franchise as prolific as its cousins. The intricate ghost featured is straight from the mind of Clive Barker, so we're in good hands. He is patient, collected, dominant, but he's out to get you despite his passive behavior. He has a hook for a hand and his M.O. is the same as Bloody Mary's, curiously.

There is no humor in this but there is gore. It is sad as much as it scary. The character arcs are tragic and the ambiance deliberately depressing; supported by a divine score that sends chills down your spine. Most other slashers had a simpler sonata, so Candyman is by default designated as the elegant type of villain, like Pinhead. The movie is minimalist but dense with authentic scares.

The actors are convincing. The neighborhood most of the action takes place in is genuinely creepy. A whole other film could spawn off the layering of its inhabitants and the way they treat the legend. This script is obviously well-polished and created in a way to kindle rare emotions in its viewer. This is the kind of horror that comes to you with no solution, no hope, and no end in sight...

7/8

CUBE

1997

Amnesic strangers awaken in a three-dimensional booby-trapped maze.

Imagine an existential slasher where the murderers are the booby-trapped cubic rooms of a futuristic and potentially alien three-dimensional labyrinth. This larger than life horror take on Rubik's cube works miracles with limited but brilliant production design that takes us out of our element and into a world of technology, traps, math, doubt, repetition, confusion and fear.

Much like its architecture, this science-fiction slasher feels like a game; like a puzzle. As such, it encourages its victim to think more than act if they want to survive. The different cubic rooms are trapped in imaginative ways to generate striking gore. The characters are amnesic and start in the cube. There is therefore little to no character exposition aside what pertains to the plot.

Cube is close to flawless. Considering its small budget, much like its heroes, the makers used their brain to come up with a gimmick that create both an illusion and a nameless subgenre that translates to "puzzle horror". Only one room was used to shoot the whole maze. The illusion is seamless! This is a mystery, so expect more questions than answers. It's part of the game...

7/8

DEEP BLUE SEA

1999

A group of scientists on an isolated research facility are attacked by sharks.

Deep Blue Sea isn't Jaws. It gets up close and personal with the shark, instead, and most of the film takes place on an isolated aquatic search facility, which makes the movie confined and claustrophobic. You can always count on Renny Harlin, director extraordinaire, for turning a horror script into an action flick. Explosions, storm, floods; you get it all.

The facility's design is dope. Its conception is puzzling. It's pretty much a tridimensional maze. Passed the point of no return, it is in constant destruction, it burns from the inside and water runs through it. All hell breaks loose. These sharks are angry and vengeful. This isn't exactly a comedy, but some of the best parts are absolutely hilarious. The story is enthralling and very dynamic.

Thomas Jane is your typical American hero. He shoots first and asks questions later. Samuel L. Jackson plays the ass hole and gets the best lines. LL Cool J is the comic relief. He's fun and sympathetic. All things considered, Deep Blue Sea may very well be one of the best killer shark movies out there. It's unpredictable, action-packed, and it's larger than life.

7/8

SLEEPY HOLLOW

1999

A constable is sent to a small town to investigate the decapitations of three people by a headless horseman.

Never would I've expected a Tim Burton period piece featuring Johnny Depp, Christina Ricci, Casper Van Dien, Christopher Walken, and Christopher Lee to be structured like a slasher film, yet here we are, with a gory, funny, and scary horror movie that defies all tropes of the genre. The budget is substantial. Sleepy Hallow is an anomaly. It's the kind of film some wish Burton made more of.

The Headless Horseman, as it turns out, is a selective monster. Part of the intrigue is figuring out what his modus operandi is. The village feels ancient, as intended, but with a hint of fantasy. There's magic in the air, beyond the headless monster. There's a witch and a tree that bleeds. Depp's character himself had a fantastic childhood, exaggerated during vivid memory sequences.

This is an adaptation loosely based on Washington Irving's 1820 short story "The Legend of Sleepy Hollow". It's sensational. It's larger than life. Danny Elfman is scoring it. What more do you want? These guys are all at their prime. The acting is impeccable. Though we never get to care much about half the characters, they are interesting enough to entertain.

7/8

CHILD'S PLAY 3

1991

A teenager joins a military college where he suspects he was found by a possessed doll that tormented him as a child.

Chucky, now a full slasher icon, finds a new child to transpose his soul into. His previous victim, Andy, is recast by an older actor. More than ever, the kills are played for a laugh at the sound of Chucky cackling. This one is much closer in tone to the sequel than to the original because the doll is fully shown and lit. He can still pull a shiver, but he's getting harder to take seriously.

We, again, see a lot of the animated wonder that is Chucky. We care less about Andy, the newly targeted kid and the rest of the military college, probably because the actors are weaker, not as well scripted and not so precisely directed. We do get an injected teenage love story, something never attempted in the franchise but a trope of pretty much every other slasher.

If you accept to trade chills for fun, cheese and one-liners, Child's Play 3 might meet most of your expectations. Sure, it's the laziest in the trilogy, takes a couple of shortcuts when it needs to move its characters from one place to another, and the finale is implausibly rushed, but as long as you suspend disbelief, you should enjoy yourself. If animatronics don't do it, the body count will.

6/8

FRANKENHOOKER

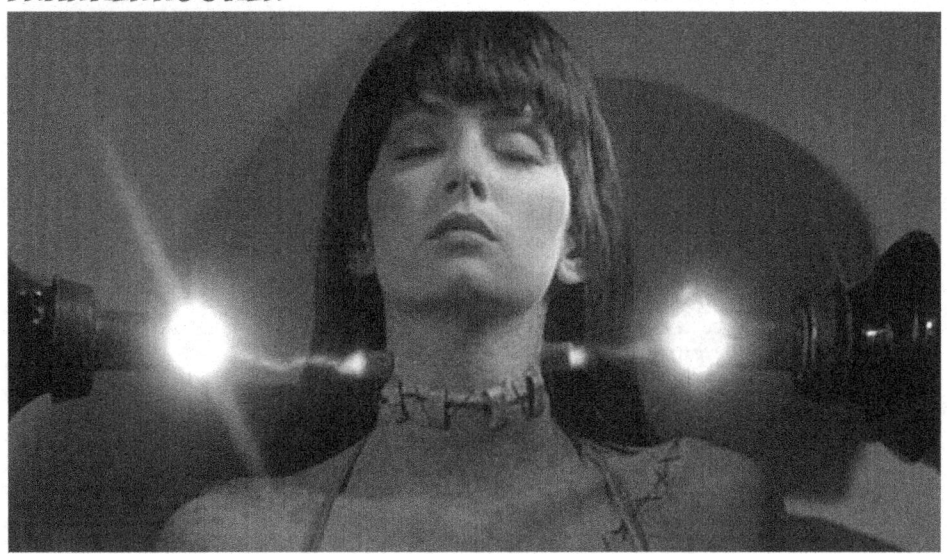

1990

A medical students attempts to re-animate his dead girlfriend using body parts from dismembered prostitutes.

This parodic take on Frankenstein is everything but old fashioned. It is nicely packaged fun, shock and macabre sprinkled with generous gratuitous nudity. Protagonist Jeffrey Franken turns himself into a mad scientist by strategically drilling holes into his brain, then attempts to mix and match body parts from different prostitutes in order to re-assemble and bring back his dead fiancée.

The film is a delightful succession of hooker jokes. It thoroughly makes fun of drug addictions, pimp clichés and the female body. It treats its gore with hilarious slapstick comedy and exaggerated practical effects. You get death by robotized lawnmower, by explosive narcotics, a dinner for two with a dismembered girlfriend and a bunch more over the top tongue-in-cheek scenes you won't forget.

There is an element of slasher to Frankenhooker. It manifests itself in the last third of the movie. Elizabeth doesn't just smack and choke her "clients"; she electrocutes them and blows them up. Her appearance, tics and M.O. make her one of the most interesting female monsters of modern horror movies. Expect an entertaining story, good reveals, twisted visuals and a memorable ending.

6/8

HELLRAISER: BLOODLINE

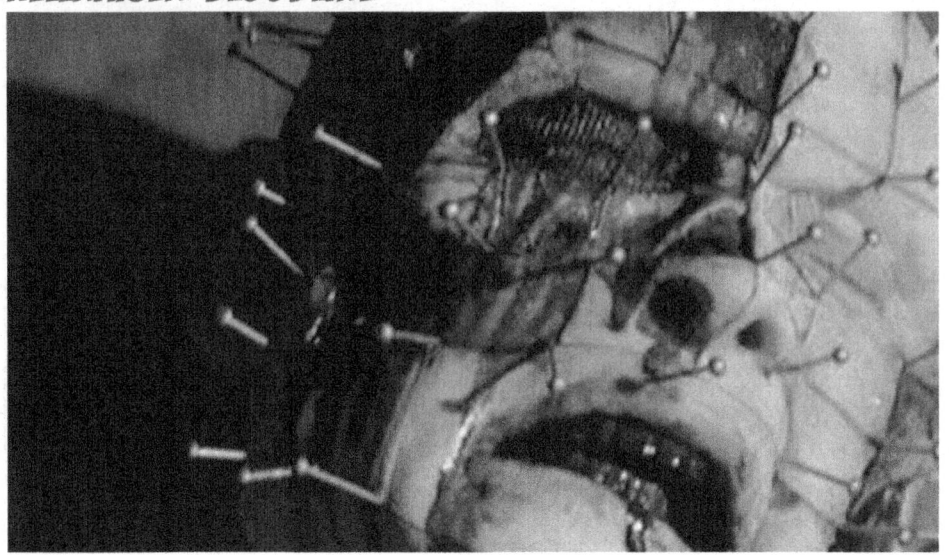

1996

Aboard a spaceship, a scientist attempts to destroy a cursed puzzle box created by his ancestor.

Traveling back and forth in time and following a dynasty of protagonists who fought Pinhead in one way or another, this movie is a prequel and a sequel at the same time. One third of the plot takes place in space. It features movable sets that it reuses plenty, but in a way to establish a merging of two worlds while saving money. The industrial lighting works well, but it's unusual for Hellraiser.

The storyline is all over the place, as if the movie was filmed in chunks with weak continuity editing and no logical transition. The angled camera gets abusive. The many particle or digital effects look cheap, but the mechanical ones and the prosthetics are some of the best the franchise has known. Pinhead has a lot of spoken lines. Sadly, he loses some of his mystery and dominance, as a result.

Some might find the film confusing; others will miss Clive Barker's sinister style from the two or three first entries. The acting is higher than average, though. The ideas thrown are all interesting; graphically and story-wise, but this one got butchered during editing or relied on it too much. The period piece backstory about the toy box and some cenobites is creative and highly entertaining.

6/8

POPCORN

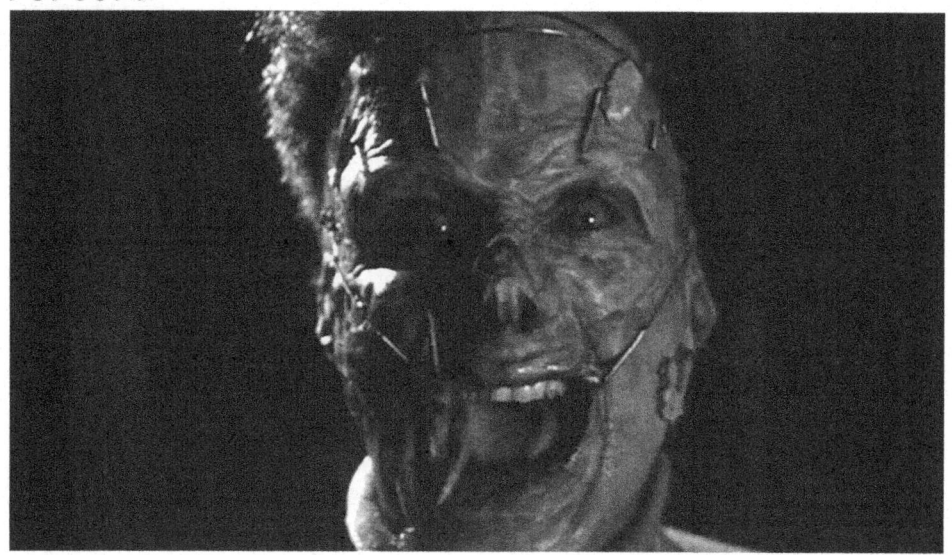

1991

A murderer kills off people at a horror movie marathon organized in an abandoned theater.

In Popcorn, a bunch of people organize an all-night horror marathon where they use old gimmicks like the Project-o-Vision, the Aroma-Rama and the Shock-o-Scope to scare, surprise or disgust their guests. Unfortunately for them, a serial killer is using their props against them and offs them one by one. Sounds fun? It's even better than words can describe.

This is a 1990's movie that belongs to the 1980's. It's atmospheric, high-spirited, it has a good vibe, at least during the exposition, it's cheesy, it's retro and it's creative. For a good while, in the first half, we have absolutely no idea what's going to happen when shit hits the fan. We understand that there is a supernatural element, but it remains vague until madness is finally unleashed.

Once it gets going, this amazing slasher never holds back. The effects are stunning, the prosthetic make-up is convincing, and the murders look painful. The most innovative element of Popcorn is that the characters are affected by the events taking place in the "movie within the movie". This is handled beautifully and is much less confusing than it sounds. Popcorn is quite the experience.

6/8

DR. GIGGLES

1992

A madman who believes he's a doctor stalks and kills random people.

We're in the early 1990's and slasher flicks are no longer trendy. Out of nowhere, this little gem comes out. It's violent, campy, sexy and marketable. It's about a wanna be doctor who uses medical tools to kill. Why hasn't this been done before? Larry Drake plays the doctor and the rest of the cast are familiar faces. Of course, all characters are paper thin, even the final girl.

So, we go from murder to murder and, just when we think this film couldn't get any cooler, we get an amusement park scene, including a murder inside a funhouse. It's short but memorable. Ten minutes before, we had teens exploring Dr. Giggles' abandoned house, just after his escape from a psychiatric institution. Geographically and chronologically, this movie is all over the place. It's hilarious.

Expect excessive gore that goes beyond what the typical slasher shows you, but then also a bunch of off-screen kills as well. There is no middle ground. If a character gets at least two minutes of exposition, in this film, they're probably going to die. Seeing as Dr. Giggles uses pretty much every medical tool someone can think of, we probably won't be getting a sequel, so enjoy it while it lasts!

HALLOWEEN H20: 20 YEARS LATER

1998

A woman who escaped a serial killer believes he son might be in danger.

We are to ignore the events of all Halloween sequels and assume they are independent from this storyline. Big budget went into this one, the script is uncluttered and it feels like a legit, classic Michael Myers movie with superior acting, photography and a vintage structure. The protagonists are likable, fully developed and display credible chemistry.

It becomes apparent, now, that simplicity was the way to go. It has always was, yet the franchise had lost itself in the details. The original movie was about teenagers getting stalked or killed, which we gradually got less of. Things became too serious, too dramatic. Tough her now manic depressive character returns, actress Jamie Lee Curtis provides an energetic presence and a great performance.

It's one of the best in the franchise. Michael Myers not being the most eccentric of horror icons, yet a frequent favorite among fans, the confined, deserted setting plays to his advantage. This is what happens when Michael Myers leaves home and invades an old building rather than a neighborhood. It's what happens when ask the cream of acting and directing to spice up a classic.

6/8

HELLRAISER III: HELL ON EARTH

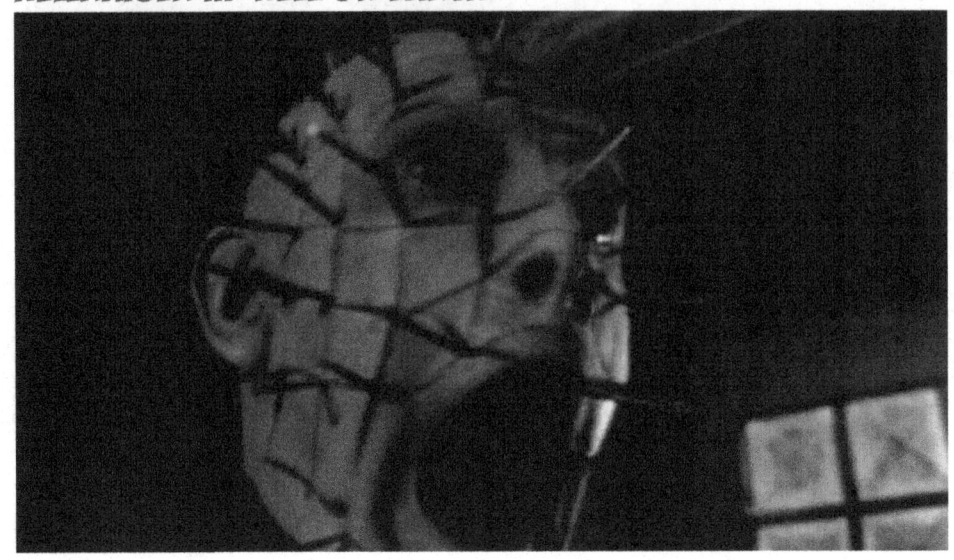

1992

A reporter investigates a man who feeds a cursed pillar human blood.

For the third time, a female protagonist gets a hold of the "lament configuration", a puzzle box that attracts a specific kind of fiend. The cenobites are now a marketing caricature of their previous self. They used to be creatures of few words and of short presence. In Hellraiser 3, they are given extended dialog, one-liners and too much backstory. You'll learn fun made-up facts about Pinhead.

This one isn't exactly artsy, nor is it reminiscent of Clive Barker's world. The first act is a refreshing take on the previous films' romantic plots; the second act is over-edited and relies too much on flashbacks, dream sequences and other post-production filler. The last act is condensed mayhem; an apocalyptic combination of funky mass slaughter, explosions, sewers blowing and cars crashing.

When you strip away the allusions to war, the journalistic procedural and the cheap plot devices, you're left with a dumbed-down and not so faithful rendition of the two first Hellraiser films with badly lit monsters, no character depth or subtlety. It is more enjoyable when it is immature than it is when it spoon-feeds us trivial information that only kill the mystery.

6/8

DISTURBING BEHAVIOR

1998

The new kid in town stumbles across something sinister about his new school.

Disturbing Behavior is a post-Scream marvel. It's comparable to The Faculty, but it struggles to live up to the blockbuster expectations of the decade. It is the ultimate high school cautionary tale, but it lacks the structure of similar slashers. It's a slasher where victims don't get killed but "converted", instead. We're talking brain implants that make students perfect; perfectly violent.

Peculiar dialogue makes Disturbing Behavior ethereal. Let's face it; Scott Rosenberg isn't Kevin Williamson. His writing, when it comes to conversation, is puzzling. Subtitles aren't a luxury, here. There is incoherence at every corner because the gimmick can barely contain itself. The bad guys are scaring everyone away while trying, ironically, to recruit them.

Think Stepford Wives. Think Invasion of the Body Snatchers. As described to the main protagonist, played by James Marsden, early on, the students are divided into five groups: the motorheads, the microgeeks, the skaters, the lames and the Blue Ribbons. This movie is a metaphor for bullying, excellence and identity. It's particularly aimed at teens, but it will hit close to home for most people.

6/8

PET SEMATARY II

1992

A man and his son move into a house located near a haunted cemetery.

There was no sign of or urgent need for a sequel to the masterpiece 1989's Pet Sematary was. It was a self-contained but dense horror story published as a novel then adapted for the screen by Stephen King. It was directed by Mary Lambert who also tackles this one. Post-production effects aside, the film looks great and gets frightening, though it never matches the eeriness felt in the original.

It has the grunge vibe of the new decade. Teen concerns and angst have replaced family drama. The protagonists are authentic, compelling and played by familiar actors who carry a sometimes wobbly but always tense script on their shoulders. By tradition, the antagonists are downright creepy. The ambiance is thick and benefits from calculated dialog, pacing, blocking, photography and camera work.

Though Pet Sematary 2 seems meant for a teen audience, it contains a generous amount of gore that feels earned and comes with consequences. Nothing is random, except perhaps the new direction taken. The most outrageous innovation, here, is that the revenants featured are smarter than depicted in 1989. Though continuity is broken, this allows for a different kind of scares.

BRIDE OF CHUCKY

1998

A woman steals a possessed doll used as evidence in a murder investigation and reanimates it using voodoo magic.

Chucky was never so funny! In fact, he was purely terrifying in the first film because his presence was only suggested during the first half, making his reveal more shocking at the moment he was fully exposed. He only gradually became the clown he is through sequels. The animatronics are now slightly better, but this is a comedy with only few scares that benefit from them.

The franchise is following its natural course. It could have taken any other tangent, but the doll is so iconic that it adopted the same route other popular horror monsters have: humor. Bride of Chucky is a strong slasher with a competent cast comprised of popular names. The performances are flawless, like most aspects of the film. The only real drawback for the fan is the lack of eeriness.

We get gore and creative kills, though. We get a new doll called Tiffany, too. Her significant entrance is marked by memorable moments that elevate her character to a status similar to Charles Lee Ray's, the serial killer who initially transferred his soul in the "Chucky" doll. This is the first time children are not a stake, but the politically correctness denatures an otherwise faithful sequel.

6/8

IDLE HANDS

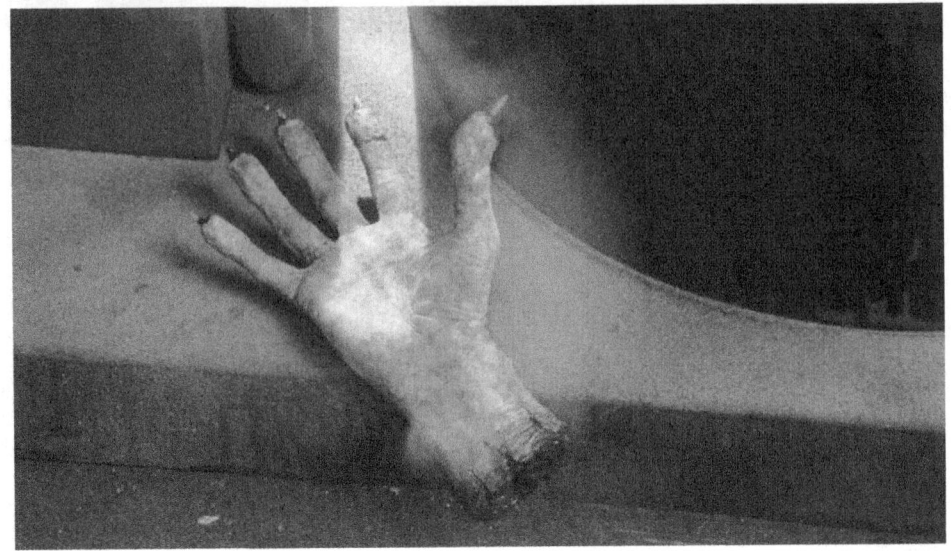

1999

A teenager's hand becomes possessed and kills.

If Evil Dead 2 didn't convince you that chopping your own hand is a dramatic thing, Ide Hands will. Idle Hands stars Devon Sawa in a career-defining role, Jessica Albas not at all presented the way girls next door usually are, and a dynamic duo composed of Seth Green and Elden Henson who get all the good lines. Vivica A. Fox is in the wrong movie and Jack Noseworthy is the creepy neighbor.

You know that a horror comedy is well orchestrated when time flies and you realize that you've reached the third act when, in fact, you thought you were barely halfway in. The humor is very dark, but it's never too dark. It's one slapstick joke after another. Sawa's character loses both parents and his best friends. He loses his hand and, still, he's that same likeable, happy-go-lucky person.

The special effects are mostly practical if you consider color-keying practical. This is an homage to horror films of the 1980's, but with a special 1990's sauce, so you basically get your pair or boobs, but you also get characters that act like real people, to a certain extent. When the jokes work, they are hysterically funny, when they don't you simply move on to the next.

6/8

1990's Slasher Films

FROM DUSK TILL DAWN 2: TEXAS BLOOD MONEY

1999

Bank robbers see their plans foiled by vampires.

In carrying the From Dusk Till Dawn, they got the tone right but visibly had a low budget and a weaker script to work with. The protagonists are still bad-ass criminals with survival skills who can give vampires a good fight. This seemed trivial until the 45 minute mark in From Dusk Till Dawn and part 2 mixes and matches these elements well. The new character dynamic gives it an interesting edge.

It's a lesser production but it's a terrific b-movie that makes the best of its resources. The sets and landscapes play a significant role in submersing the audience and the actors do a great job. Comedy, drama, crime and supernatural all merge into one, as they did so brilliantly in part 1. Subgenres alternate constantly and each bit is as fun as the previous. Of course, you get gore, too.

The "Titty Twister", revealed to be a vampire nest disguised as a stripped club in the previous twist, is reintroduced but is no longer is at the center of the story. This is more about a bank robbery gone terribly wrong and, more importantly, the preceding over the top character exposition. The effects are sometimes cheap, the last act is somewhat weak, but it's still a solid sequel.

6/8

KOLOBOS

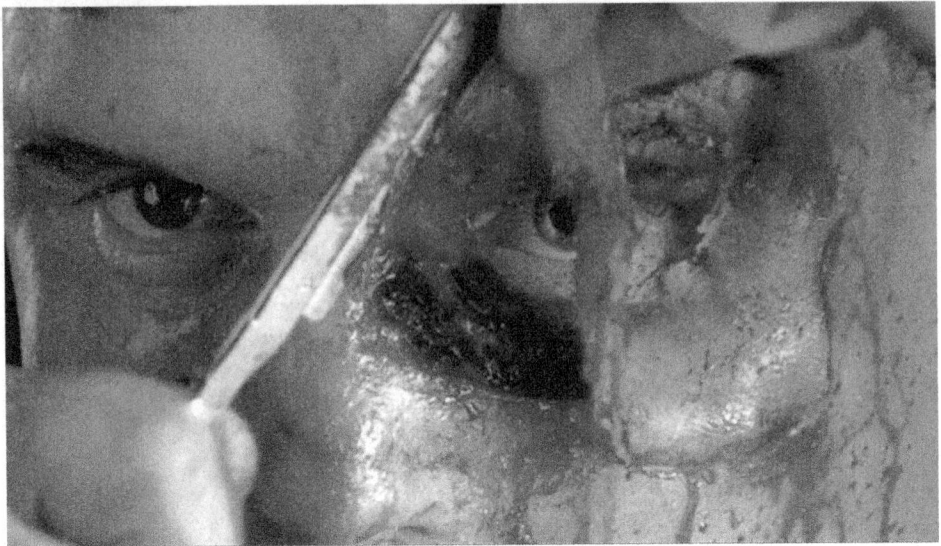

1999

A house dedicated to a reality show is suddenly locked down with a mass murderer inside.

It's 1999. Everyone's watching Big Brother on TV. Scream was released three years prior and, some would agree, it was one of the best slasher films ever made. Kolobos banks on the zeitgeist. These influences are all over. But Kolobos, as it turns out, would inspire countless films in the 2000's. As such, it is an underdog. It is a pioneer in the puzzle horror subgenre.

The plot somewhat occurs out of chronological order, a trend that is gaining in popularity. This may or may not benefit us in the long run. The ambiance is intoxicating, which is attributable to two directors who truly care. They want to give us an experience. We're introduced to protagonists we instantly love. If they're going to die horribly, we should at least get to know them first.

They are well-groomed. Most of them come with a positive, bubbly attitude, but Kyra has the kind of baggage that hints at a complicated subplot. The dialogue is fun, effervescent, but unnatural. At the halfway mark, the creators show their best and weakest cards. The screenplay, then, becomes polarized and far-fetched. There's gore, there's screaming, and terror ensues.

6/8

PREDATOR 2

1990

A police officer discovers that the drug lords he is after are being decimated by an invisible creature.

We leave the jungle of 1987's Predator and now find ourselves in a dystopian Los Angeles undergoing gang wars. Arnold Schwarzenegger has been replaced by a less spectacular Danny Glover, but the quality of the cast meets the standards. This is still horror and science-fiction with the narrative structure of an action flick, something that stood out the first time around.

The procedural never gets in the pacing's way. This is a fast movie. Expect lots of ridiculous explosions, car chases, blood and, of course, big guns. While this is presented as urban fantasy, we couldn't be further from real life in regards to set design. The film is heavily textured. The exterior shots are post-apocalyptic and the interior ones are reminiscent of the pyramids of Ancient Egypt.

They sure didn't shy on the gore and made the alien race even more viscerally brutal. They threw in a twist or two. Sadly, some of the digital effects are deplorable; mainly because the creators' ambition surpasses their technology. This sequel succeeds at innovation, isn't mere repetition, but it could have benefited from more contrasting and sensationalized characters.

6/8

PSYCHO

1998

A woman steals a large sum of money from her employer and hides in a motel owned by a mysterious man.

This is a shot by shot remake of Alfred Hitchcock's classic thriller by the same name. An unaware audience might wonder why it feels so much like a period piece, and others why it was made in the first place. The true reason is mostly copyright-driven but, for all intents and purposes, this can be useful to the film student or simply to the fan who wants a modern color rendition.

As a stand-alone film, it is almost as appreciable as the original, but times have changed and so have morals. The story is only timeless in and around the infamous motel. Some taboos are approached with an upgraded eye and as a wink to those who found 1960's version subversive. On the surface, this is just another romantic thriller. Psycho only gains depth around the mid-point.

From that moment on, things get tense; as tense as Hitchcock managed to be. 1998's Psycho is most enjoyable if compared to a play with a story so good it is being retold and extrapolated. 1990's sequel wasn't great and this comes as a pleasant surprise for the completist. It's a collection piece as much as a nod to the master of suspense. It's a grand film in the shadow of a grander film.

6/8

SLEEPWALKERS

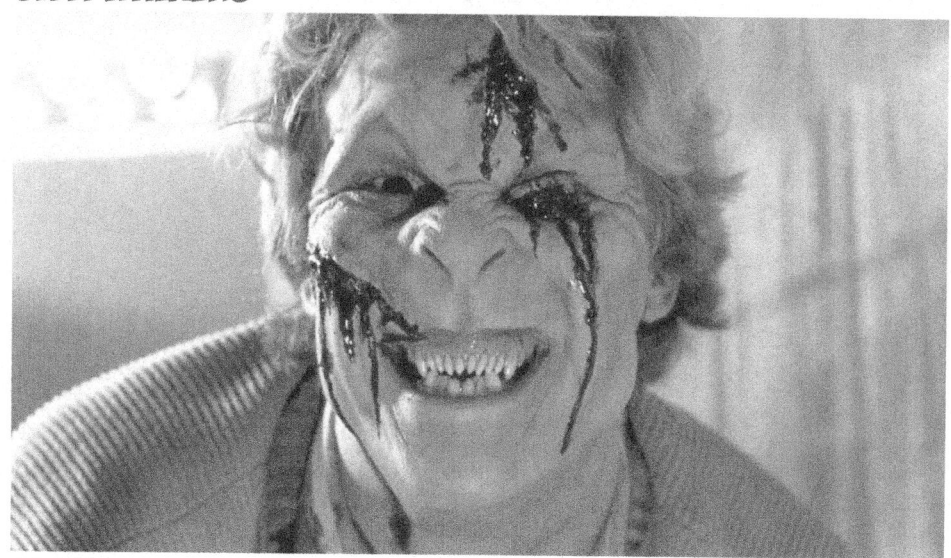

1992

Two lycanthropes move to a small town to seek out a young virgin to feed on.

The three main characters, in Sleepwalkers, get fabulous introductions. One is shirtless, another one is trapping cats, and the third one, our protagonist, is dancing in the empty theater she works at while cleaning the floor. Sleepwalkers is one of the most musical Stephen King stories. It is directed by one of his most prolific adaptors; Mick Garris, and this is one of his best efforts.

The screenplay is daring. Its flaws make the film charming. It's not particularly clever. It is controversial. It deals with subjects like rape and incest with a tongue-in-cheek approach. There is a discrepancy between what Brian Krause's character thinks of his crush, and what he attempts to do to her once they finally date. It's a pivotal moment in the film's structure and it's badly handled.

Sleepwalkers' casting is impressive. Mädchen Amick is so gorgeous her beauty is practically part of the plot. She plays the virgin those two werecats need. The antagonists are similar to vampires, by design, and they need her vital energy. Things are never explained to us in those words, though. Indeed, this film is more oriented towards atmosphere than substance. It's kind of a slasher, too!

6/8

I KNOW WHAT YOU DID LAST SUMMER

1997

Four teenagers receive death threats from an anonymous writer one year after having hit a stranger with their car.

This movie piggybacks on the success of Scream. This metro-sexual slasher comes out one year after its cousin, but feels like a lesser version of it. The intrigue leads to a revelation that can't live up to better plausible slashers. The lead actors do a convincing job with the superficial dialog they are given. They are some of the best of their generation and the main attraction, here.

Some might recognize an underlying pattern that will remind them of the Hookman urban legend. The villain has a hook for a hand and the plot revolves around disturbed love stories, but the parallels stop there. IKWYDLS doesn't always know what it wants to be. It implicitly invites us to try and guess the killer's identity, but eventually gives up red herrings and neglects its final reveal.

The body count is surprisingly low and gore isn't the focus; disorderly teen relationships are. Some subplots feel stretched, far-fetched, and do not contribute much to the course of the story. The novel this is based on is only vaguely similar, but is also aimed at a younger crowd. This is a good gateway horror movie with a strong social layer that succeeds in making us care for its characters.

6/8

GRAVEYARD SHIFT

1990

A cleaning crew disinfects the basement of an old textile mill infested with rats.

Graveyard Shift, adaptation of a short story by Stephen King, is hard to summarize. It's about a handful of workers doing an impossible job, working overtime under the supervision of the worst boss ever written in a screenplay. Stephen Macht plays the bastard. David Andrews plays a low-key protagonist and Brad Dourif an excessive exterminator. Kelly Wolf plays everybody's love interest. Awkward!

Nothing about Graveyard Shift is perfect. The dialogue is more amusing than it is clever. The matte painting never achieves an illusion but creates a deep atmosphere. The monster doesn't make sense, but it's an excellent source of gore. This film would be a complete disaster if the creators weren't so damn talented. This is not your run-of-the-mill horror picture. It's way better than that.

Like most scary movies that play their cards right, this one would be a good drama if you removed the horror elements from it. It would be the story of Warwick, an ass hole, and his shitty business. What happens in the basement, when the exploration starts, is reminiscent of Alien and Aliens. Graveyard Shift, then, turns into a big, dumb and dark adventure flick. This one is a no brainer.

6/8

ALIEN: RESURRECTION

1997

The host of an alien parasite is cloned by her former employer's scientists.

The fine set design successfully matches the dark metallic vibe of the established franchise, but we're taking a steampunk approach not unlike Alien 3. The effects are arguably the worst they've been; shown in moderation because the beasts are mere 3D meshes. Sigourney Weaver's character is brought back to life by a crazy plot device that we are invited to accept for continuity's sake.

In this one, the aliens are treated like cattle and serve as backdrop to a bunch of tough guys. The characters act as a group of space adventurers with each their skills and gadgets, this movie taking place much further in the future. It's also efficiently setup as a slasher movie, as it always was, but with frantic camera work and exaggerated photography.

It's interesting to see the creatures under captivity, vulnerable, and studied. This shows us just how animalistic, yet tactical they are. When they escape, it's up to a revitalizing cast of colorful heroes to clear the place. Ripley now adopts alien mannerism, having inherited part of their DNA; a clever decision that somewhat justifies her character's physical and moral resilience...

6/8

PUPPET MASTER II

1991

A collection of possessed puppets collect human tissue for their master to help create a formula that brings back the dead.

This sequel isn't as artsy and is a bit more accessible than the original Puppet Master. It is still a visionary supernatural horror b-movie, and still takes place in that majestic Victorian hotel, but it goes out of its way and its limited location to push the gimmick a little further. It picks up where we left off and almost remakes itself.

The characters are deeper, more plausible and not all so overwhelmingly eccentric. It's a good sequel but it's definitely more of the same done a little better and with more background story. It's great to see those memorable puppets come back to life, once more, and be given more screen time. They are the center of this, after all. Cool hybrids and a toy robot join their universe.

The special effects aren't terrific but they are a vast improvement. The riggers and puppeteers surpassed themselves since the original. The character of Toulon, master of puppets, has a great visual design and a rich story arc that complements what we already know about him as a monster. The slasher vibe has been reinforced by clichés but it works in the film's advantage.

5/8

PROM NIGHT III: THE LAST KISS

1990

A college student helps a ghost exact revenge on those responsible for her death.

The first Prom Night was a whodunit slasher with a simple story and actors abnormally big for a production of the type. The first sequel introduced a strong, funky supernatural element that proved successful despite a cast mostly unknown. Part 3 also takes this path, but is more superficial about its ambiance, its scares, its gore and the taboos it tackles.

What was kinky is now vanilla and what was dark is now amusing more than it is frightening. As a trademark, Mari Lou Maloney, the antagonist, still spits out one-liners coined in the 50's. She has been recast and it drills another hole in continuity, sadly. It's a shame because this movie, like the two previous ones, can be summed up as quintessential horror but not as part of a whole.

Where Part 2 had a case of possession, this one depicts a manipulative affectional and sexual bond between a human and a ghost; in some cases with the straightest of faces. Ironically, this is the film's main attraction. Suspending disbelief may in fact lead you to love this hidden gem more than initially expected. The effects aren't all great, but the pace is effective and the story captivating.

5/8

LEPRECHAUN 3

1995

In Las Vegas, a broke gambler steals a leprechaun's gold and suffers its wrath.

Considering where the franchise has been and where it could go after the last feature, transporting the plot it to Las Vegas is not that big a stretch. The nonsensical leprechaun gimmick makes the two first films runner-ups in a world of better horror icons, and this new installment attempts to raise the bar higher in terms of imaginatively, script cohesion, and character writing.

The first elephant in the room is the Tammy character, played with a straight face by Lee Armstrong, who spends a good while partially nude to accommodate the Las Vegas setting and to keep us interested. The other actors are also invested despite their ridiculous part. Ironically, this is the best Leprechaun film to date and those oddities are in fact the flick's accidental charm and style.

It can be called sexist, misogynist, but then doesn't treat its men much better. It's colorful, innocent, titillating, sexual, kinky, the photography is vivid and the effects increasingly ambitious. A subplot involves the main protagonist getting infected by a leprechaun bite and turning into one, a device that belongs to zombie films and that only clusters the mythology in this case.

5/8

WWW.TERROR.CA

PUPPET MASTER III: TOULON'S REVENGE

1991

During World War II, Nazis murder the wife of a puppeteer who can transfer souls into inanimate objects.

We knew these puppets had some connection to Nazi history. This sequel attempts to explain how and why and there are pleasant surprises along the way. It's a period piece, a prequel and it contains clever twists you probably won't see coming. The sensitive Holocaust material is well-handled. Furthermore, it's a clever plot device that introduces the concept of research on eternal life.

Sumptuous Gothic sets are used as backdrop, but this time we're in Berlin during World War II and threats are everywhere. The puppets are no longer answering to a villain but a hero, now. The Nazis are the antagonists and the puppets follow Andre Toulon's directives. We actually follow the old tortured man throughout the movie. It's quite the mental gymnastics, indeed, but it works.

This is the most polished movie in this franchise at this point. The quality of the screenplay, the effects, the dialog and the cinematography are upped a notch. The actors do a good job, too. Puppet Master 3's only drawback is that it isn't scary. It is starting to feel like a cartoon and is losing its evil signature, but it's entertaining all the same.

5/8

WISHMASTER

1997

A genie attempts to grant its owner three wishes in order open a gateway to his dimension.

This throwback at 80's horror borrows from many classics and creates a hybrid curiously left underexploited in a decade of gimmicks: the genie, or "Djinn". This gorefest has a unique villain with an amusing and ironic M.O. He is more a magician than a brute and will therefore appeal to supernatural slasher fans. He basically perverts your spoken desires in ways to kill you in creative ways.

The Djinn is scary because he murders his victims by conversing. When he takes the appearance of a human, as he does for most of the running time, he becomes inconspicuous and inquisitive. The writers have him use subterfuges and twists on words to get people to wish out loud, which obviously comes with comedy. While ridden with cliches, Wishmaster ventures in unfamiliar spheres of terror.

Dream sequences and flashbacks bring the movie down. The only thing this homage to a better era does wrong, when trying to go retro, is indulging in compositing and digital editing. New technologies should be a strength; not a hindrance. Many horror legends play more or less significant roles, but costume, production and set design never do them justice, making this somewhat a sad testament.

5/8

WWW.TERROR.CA

WISHMASTER 2: EVIL NEVER DIES

1999

An evil genie hunting for souls is put in prison while in human form.

This franchise doesn't waste a minute on continuity, shamelessly getting rid of Robert Englund, Kane Hodder, Tony Todd and every other actor having played a major 80's horror movie monster. It trades it all for Andrew Divoff, second tier icon in the genre, and a prison setting, though it does things right in regards to its gimmick by putting all the focus on tampered wishes.

Part 1 had an awesomely gory introduction that this sequel can't match and won't even try to. Like most scenes, it feels isolated, rushed and engineered to facilitate whatever special effect can be afforded. Divoff seizes the Djinn part and makes it his own, though he fights a regrettable faked accent he's stuck with. He is somewhat treated like a protagonist and is given many horrendous lines.

Jack Sholder writes and directs with many limitations, including his own. He can't come up with the right words to make dialog flow, namely; no more than he can write a two way discussion that naturally and seamlessly leads to a formulated wish and therefore to death. As a supernatural slasher, it does a lot of things right. As a sequel, it's a huge deception.

5/8

CHILDREN OF THE CORN III: URBAN HARVEST

1995

Unbeknownst to their new adoptive parents, two young members of a demonic cult intend to infiltrate a city.

Something had to be done to spice things up. The franchise has been too rigid, emotionally absent, and the last film barely had any interesting effects. There's only so much story to be told around haunted corn fields and Children of the Corn 3 therefore moves its intrigue to the big city. Because the cultists have dropped in number, this one in fact borrows a lot from the evil kid subgenre.

Some of the effects are a vast improvement over the previous two films and the lasting image of a corn field growing around an apartment building opens up a world of screenwriting possibilities. The frequent use of creeping plants as antagonists summarizes where we've taken this series. Although entertainingly cheesy, it is also a confession that the franchise's potential is already running dry.

It is the first of the Children of the Corn movies to fully embrace its slasher potential. The kill count is higher and the gore abundant. The makers, aware that the premise is silly, choose to deliver something crazy, fun; making the best of the intricate supernatural threat. The practical effects are well crafted and animated. They are seemingly reminiscent of horror classics of the 1980's.

NIGHT OF THE DEMONS III

1997

On Halloween night, teenage misfits take refuge in an empty house haunted by demons.

Night of the Demons was representative of its decade, and this new sequel struggles to find its spot in evolution. Instead of taking the plot to a new location suitable for a Halloween night of partying, an interesting twist catches us off guard early on and creates a quadruple threat: death, possession, a detective and a bully. Most of the story unravels in Hull House again.

The demons are only one of the many categories of antagonists in this sequel. It's a little much for a franchise based off simple storytelling. The last thing we needed was a subgenre mashup. Night of the Demons 1 & 2 had memorable exposition and were known for incessant tongue in cheek humor. Here, though, the mood is not innocent and neither are the protagonists we should relate to.

Part 3 is faithful to the original when it comes to presenting awkward performances, cheese, gore and boobs. Latex has been replaced by CG and it looks fake. Make-up isn't great. A lot of the original essence is lost. It's not very scary, not very funny, and, mostly, the directing isn't keen. The camera is all over the place and tilted in crazy angles that can't compensate for bad set design.

5/8

URBAN LEGEND

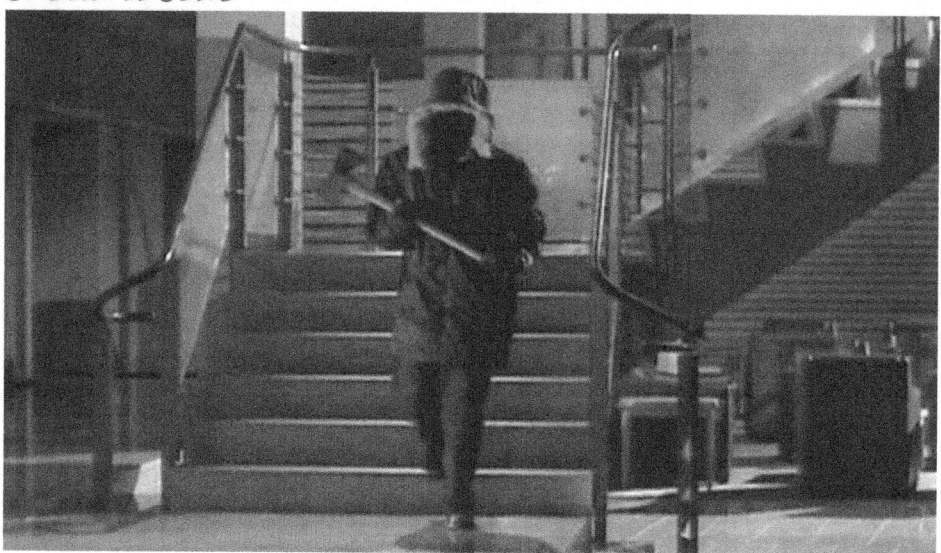

1998

College students are targeted by a serial killer who replicates urban legends.

Scream polished the slasher genre and gave it a new life. The creators of Urban Legend hop on the glamour bandwagon with a masked killer whose M.O. is inspired by common urban legends and campfire tales. Urban Legends knows its place in the subgenre and in history but makes the partially rehashed premise its own. While the tone is familiar, social behaviors aren't the same, for one thing.

There are big names attached to this, including actors who marked horror fans of a generation; Robert Englund, Brad Dourif and Daniel Harris, precisely. Jared Leto, Rebecca Gayheart, Joshua Jackson and Tara Reid are a strong and lively ensemble. We are asked to care about them until they succumb, but the film also throws red herring, implying the killer might be one of them. Sounds familiar?

This plausible but improbable whodunit is well written but dumbed down for a young or reminiscing audience that agrees to leave part of their brain at the door and enjoys thorough character development. This is a sitcom approach to horror that wasn't a thing in the 80's. The murders usually occur in contexts and places that end up stretching well-earned suspense rather than pure gore.

5/8

JASON GOES TO HELL: THE FINAL FRIDAY

1993

An immortal assassin gains the ability to transfer his soul from one individual to the next.

Jason was in fact his mother, then he had a copycat. In the 7th film, he faced a girl with psychic abilities, only to end up in New York City in the sequel prior to this one. We push the envelope further, here, giving the famous horror icon the power to move his soul from body to body. Copyright technicalities are the reason for it. As a result, we barely get to see Jason in his classic design.

This movie breaches continuity and the ambiance initiated by the original then maintained by the previous ones. It rushes through forced teenage exposition, nudity, gives us an older cast, frantic protagonists, and a horrendous, unnecessary backstory that doesn't even address our questions, if any. We've established that Jason is a supernatural being, but a demon parasite? Really?

While the cinematography and performances are arguably the best they've been, and while the gore is entertainingly abundant, the plot is drilled with nonsense. The finale has a great build-up, but half our expectation is caused by the delaying of important elements. It's fast paced, very dynamic, and comparable to a dark comic book. It should be seen despite the flaws of the script.

5/8

THE LAWNMOWER MAN

1992

A simple man is turned into a mad genius by virtual reality.

The virtual reality in this film absolutely doesn't stand the test of time. The 3-D world is poorly conceived and constitutes a significant part of the story. Pierce Brosnan and Jeff Fahey partially redeem this weird production with their performances. Their characters develop an interesting win-win relationship. One needs a guinea pig; the other a higher IQ.

You'll need to suspend disbelief to swallow this movie whole. The science fiction, here, is a lot to take in. This story may work on paper but doesn't translate so well on screen. The Lawnmower Man was loosely inspired by a short story written by Stephen King. King rejected the credit and here we are, with a bastard but captivating, eccentric and unique product.

Jeff Fahey's character's transformation is the central element of interest. He slowly merges with the virtual world, imagining things and seeing with a new pair of eyes. He becomes psychic. He slowly turns evil as he gets smarter and addicted to "the machine". If you can see through the bad effects the intents of the writer, you might just enjoy yourself, here. Just don't get your hopes too high.

5/8

I STILL KNOW WHAT YOU DID LAST SUMMER

1998

An avenging hook-wielding murderer chases down a couple on vacation in the Bahamas.

The original film was loosely based off a novel and vaguely combined with a popular urban legend. It piggy backed on 1996's Scream's revolutionary way of marketing a horror production and alluded to a whodunit formula. As revealed in the twist, it was in fact not a whodunit despite many red herrings, but a man whose face was never shown during the two first acts. I Still Know plays the same card.

Jennifer Love Hewitt returns as the lovable final girl and Freddie Prinze Jr as his absent boyfriend. The cast looks as superficially good as the previous one. ISKWYDLS defines the quintessential high-end slasher of the era. The arc is carried from the fishing town of Part 1 to the Bahamas using a ludicrous plot device that seems forced but that the bubbly actors make easier to accept.

The backdrops are gorgeous when bathing in day light and oppositely scary at night. Lighting is handled to perfection, though more time should have been spent in the wild to take full advantage of a script that instead spends it on convoluted ideas. This is a high budget production with many audiences to please, cleavage to show and singers to promote. It's as commercial as horror gets!

5/8

THE DENTIST

1996

An obsessive compulsive cuckolded dentist starts torturing his clients.

You can't have a slasher film with a dentist for a villain without gore. The writers knew this all too well and put their effort on striking gore and what leads to it. Brian Yuzna and Stuart Gordon have similar styles and have been known for their stability in horror cinema. One is writing and the other directing here. Both have a way to deliver good stories on low to medium budgets seamlessly.

The mad dentist is often subject to delirium and hallucinations caused by a trademark obsessive compulsive behavior. The idea is interesting on paper but the experimental effects attempted meet a common pitfall of the decade. The compositing is bad and makes use of skewing; a flat two-dimensional effect that is easy to create but breaks the 4th wall. This should never make the final cut.

Dialog is never a form of filler and ambiance takes care of the slower moments. This film isn't big on suspense because the dentist is introduced as the main protagonist so we can see evil and decay from his perspective. When that's out of the way, the story takes an unexpected tangent that pays off in the third act. From then on, build-up is possible and handled beautifully.

5/8

PSYCHO IV: THE BEGINNING

1990

A psychopathic murderer confesses his story to a radio host.

Antony Perkins returns and shares his legendary character with two young actors. This is Norman Bates' backstory. We toggle between his childhood and teenage memories in order to learn about his mother's illness and his own. Perkins narrates on and off-screen so as not to lose the original essence. This time, his madness is not questioned and real answers are provided.

We learn about his first kill. We also learn what we suspected: Mother smothered and molested Norman. Their relationship is awkward and challenges us to keep watching. We knew Norman had mommy issues, but seeing the emerging damage is troubling. Loyal to the legacy, director Mick Garris uses ambiguity to censor his own work and provides nothing more than safe scares and good suspense.

The incest scenes suggest consent from both parties. It makes the story layered but heavy, considering Norman Bates is the protagonist. As a late sequel, Psycho 4 is a cost-effective shenanigan that has Perkins talking on the phone alone in a kitchen; as a prequel, it goes deep into the sometimes unnecessary details of his madness. By casting nobodies, the rest of the film feels more organized.

5/8

THE DARK HALF

1993

A writer is losing control of his fictional alter ego.

This is another horror story about a tormented writer by Stephen King. It is directed by George A. Romero, so technically we're in good hands. It's about a man who may or may not be responsible for a series of murders. Enough clues are exposed so that, by the end of the first act, if we really think this through, there can only be so many solutions to the mystery. It's kind of obvious...

The Dark Half's main strength is that it is imaginative enough while remaining simple. It's about a family man afflicted by what seems like a supernatural curse. However remarkable his story may be, the film is mostly treated like a procedural thriller. The characters are sympathetic. The casting comes out naturally. Let's face it, though, the ultimate reveal doesn't make sense.

The elephant in the room is the twist itself. It's a gaping plot hole and it can't be spoiled. The best thing about The Dark Half is that it is a good slasher. Once it gets going, it's nothing but a streak of cool looking murders by razor blade. The killer is creepy. The kills are gruesome. The film is as good as it could be with this type of story, and most of it is due to excellent directing.

5/8

ALIEN3

1992

A stowaway alien causes a space traveler's ship to crash on a planet inhabited by human prisoners.

First, our leads were officers, then a military force, and now they're some cult emerging among dangerous unarmed prisoners on a dystopian planet. Played by Sigourney Weaver, Ripley returns as the only female in a male dominated film. Her arrival stirs up tensions. It's good to see some context, wisdom and humanity injected into the franchise. This is the more spiritual and emotional Alien.

While we're used to sets of spaceship interiors, here we get a rudimentary prison with a labyrinthine configuration. Some rooms look right out of our planet and our time, as if to depict a primitive world despite the science-fiction. The CG looks very bad for such a strong product. It's a shame. Maybe this is why the dialog is so poignantly extended, and why we see so little of the actual beast...

Ripley finally gets a moment of rest, of sex, shows her feminine side and her motherly qualities more than ever. This second Alien sequel does her character justice by giving her a well-deserved though late character development. Many scenes are filmed in a grime environment. The sets are matched in quality, but the style and ambiance are something else and can get pretentiously artsy.

5/8

SPECIES II

1998

An astronaut infected by an alien parasite returns from Mars and attempts to procreate.

Eve was a terrific seducer. She was a pretext for nudity and gore but handled her part as she was meant; seizing the audience with her cold beauty. She returns and finds her equivalent in a male counterpart. He makes her a protagonist, by default, and poses a challenge to her. He is both the enemy and an object of desire. While this gives them depth, it mostly nullifies the scare factor.

By siding with a supernatural being, we don't scare easy but can still be shocked. This film is gory and creative at it. It has no shame getting into threesome territory and other sexual deviances. Species 2, much like the original, calls upon our most basic instincts, but with surprisingly high quality standards that translates into above average acting, photography, pacing and screenwriting.

The signature fun vibe is nowhere to be found. Skin doesn't always feel earned. The leads simply don't have comedy in them; not even tongue-in-cheek. All aspects considered, this is a sequel that deserves its title. It brings back enough elements from the first film to ensure continuity and lets the story evolve as it should using elements that were left untouched the first time around.

5/8

FROM DUSK TILL DAWN 3: THE HANGMAN'S DAUGHTER

1999

In Old West, a group of outlaws face a vampire infestation.

This is the western version of a concept that already felt like it was homage to the genre, but with a modernized crime subplot. Like the two previous films, things only start out "gangster" to surprise a now warned audience with a midpoint twist and a toggled subgenre: horror. This sudden switch was pretext for shared directorial collaboration in part 1 and is the only thing that matters.

The story is fun to sit through, faithful to the original script and feels like a continuous trilogy conclusion, of which it is a prequel. The make-up is not as good as you would expect, and the compositing isn't much better. For this reason, we tend to fall back on the actors who are given challenging characters as eccentric as those so carefully fleshed out in the previous installments.

Things get a little of out hand during the last act. Misuse of visuals and botched editing end up ruining the pace, mystery and suspense we invested ourselves in. It minimizes the impact the final shooting location should have. By the time the credits roll, we do have more background on the vampire nest, but we still don't have answers to questions asked by From Dusk Till Dawn's shocking ending...

5/8

LEPRECHAUN

1993

A banished leprechaun set free by mistake hunts down those who steal his gold coins.

Most holidays have been exploited by the horror genre, at this point, but St-Patrick's Day had mostly been left untouched. It at least never had a slasher icon associated with it and Leprechaun fills the void with a creature design almost as interesting as Freddy Krueger's or Jason Voorhees'. The evil elf, played by Warwick Davis, is an aggregation of hilarious Irish cliches and speaks in rhymes.

The protagonists are of different generations, so everybody gets his scare. As is the case with most horror movies endangering a child that is smarter than everybody else, we don't fully invest ourselves because we know nothing bad will happen to them. And we're right... Jennifer Aniston plays a generic survivor girl that struggles with her dialog but seems comfortable despite the ludicrous premise.

Leprechaun has a catchy sonata, magical powers and a mythos adapted to common horror tropes. Eventually, the movie turns into a mad circus and an endless chase around a small house. It isn't scary but doesn't try to be. It's campy, dark in places and lively in others. It isn't exactly the masterpiece its famous horror cousins were, but it is unique enough to generate a franchise.

5/8

PUMPKINHEAD II: BLOOD WINGS

1994

Inhabited by the soul of a dead deformed child, an avenging demon is awakened by a bunch of teenagers.

In order to bring back the elements we liked from Part 1 while avoiding redundancy, it was decided, by the writers, that a bunch of clumsy teenagers were to run over the witch from the original movie, triggering a familiar series of events. Improbable but convenient, this plot device is the best thing they could've come up with. The new material is then both fresh and reminiscent.

If you enjoy 80's cheese and its typical slasher vibe, then this is for you. The only thing missing, here, is actor Lance Henrisken. He isn't returning but the script doesn't need him anyway. Better lit, better shot, filled with comic reliefs and with a slightly different ambiance, this sequel has a soul of its own. This said, it contains too many flashback sequences ruining the pacing.

Clearly, Pumpkinhead is a man in a suit, but it is creepy nonetheless and the illusion works because the puppetry is great. The gore is dramatic and so is the lighting in moments of tension, making Pumpkinhead terribly imposing. You need to watch this movie if you liked the previous one, because a lot of effort clearly went into satisfying the fans.

5/8

MOSQUITO

1994

Human-sized mutated mosquitoes force park rangers and robbers to band together in a fight for survival.

This film has the appeal of a 1950's creature feature with the approach of a 1980's slasher. This is both good and bad news, depending on your mood and your patience threshold. Dumb park rangers and other equally dumb characters come and go. Then again, this is a movie about giant alien mosquitoes. The mosquitoes look fake. They're a mix of bad puppetry, color keying, and stop motion.

Director Gary Jones keeps centering his subjects and doesn't know how to make dialogue flow dynamically, let alone organically. A lot of this film is shot in daylight, and under a grey sky. It's daunting. The night shots are far more interesting, photographically. The kills are very graphic and are the best part of this crapfest. Now, the film isn't all terrible. Give it time.

Mosquito is lengthy, considering what it has to say. It could've ended half way through and I would've been satisfied. It decided to invest in ludicrous subplots, and despite its flaws and its redundancy, I still had fun. Gunnar Hansen has a significant role and ends up fighting mosquitoes with a chainsaw in a scene right out of Night of the Living Dead. Doesn't get better than this!

5/8

MANIAC COP 3: BADGE OF SILENCE

1993

The body of a vengeful cop is reanimated by a sorcerer.

Visually, it's the most interesting of the three. It feels like the one with the highest budget. The make-up effects are better, the actors feel at ease. The protagonist from the Maniac Cop 2 is once again featured, as he must face, once more, the unstoppable revenant policeman.

The kills are getting a little more creative and overkill, something known in the slasher world, but something new in this franchise. The evil cop is more iconic than ever with his large silhouette, his strong build and his military mannerism. The better photography and sound give him even more presence.

His motivation for killing is running thin, so don't expect an excellent script. They had to tie the revenant to a Wiccan and a curse that allows him to cheat death, once more. Here is the best depiction, so far, of the horror icon that likes guns and car chases.

5/8

PINOCCHIO'S REVENGE

1996

An attorney acquires a wooden puppet from a condemned serial killer and gives it to her daughter.

For a horror movie about a possessed wooden puppet, Pinocchio's Revenge sure beats around the bush. The subplots stack up, and we hope we'll get to see the thing move some time before the end credits. Pinocchio is the poor man's Chucky. It's barely articulated. It has a weak design. Also, its never lies and its nose, therefore, never technically stretches.

So, if you're a completist of evil doll films, you need to see this. It's an ambitious picture. What it lacks visually, it compensates for with decent acting and lingering mystery. It doesn't protect its twist ending particularly well. In fact, this is one the most predictable plot twists ever. It's so badly rendered that it pretty much destroys the story and its potential for sequels.

Sometimes, the things you don't see are scarier. Well this doesn't apply here. Pinocchio's Revenge could be so much more colorful, gorier, and terrifying if it didn't keep its antagonist in the dark, and if less occurred off-screen. This one probably worked better on paper, because the end result leaves much to be desired. Good concept; bad execution.

5/8

UNCLE SAM

1996

A war veteran who was killed in combat rises from the grave on Independence Day.

If there's one thing filmmaker Larry Cohen will be remembered for, it's executing ludicrous concepts with a straight face. William Lustig is directing and he, too, has quite the resume. This film isn't half as silly as its premise. "Uncle Sam" is a revenant, to get technical. He was a soldier once, and he's some kid's undead uncle, now, hence the title. Clever.

The commentary is strong, and hammered, yet the message isn't clear. Are we pro-war, or against it? Is Uncle Sam liberally inclined or the other way around? All in all, I think it's about military wisdom. It's not black and white. The script avoids the pitfalls of divisive political subjects. Now, forty minutes in, this thing turns into a full-fledged juvenile slasher, and that's all that counts.

All the subtext in the world can't buy a good slasher. And when it gets going, it's one murder after another. The murders have a patriotic flavor. I wasn't sure about this film, initially, but, as it developed, it got my full attention. There are ups and downs, but, as a whole, this one hits all the right notes. This story takes place around Independence Day, of course.

WARLOCK: THE ARMAGEDDON

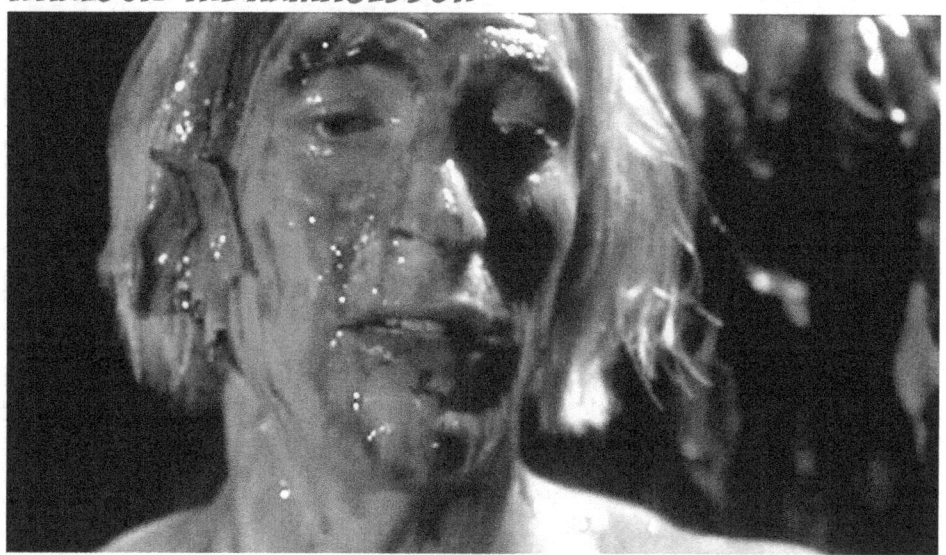

1993

An order of druids train their offspring to fight an evil wizard.

An amazing but shocking birth scene sets the tone for a film even more intense than the first one was. The wizard, in Warlock 2, is nothing less than the son of Satan. It is up to a bunch of people, descendants of druids, and possibly jedi, too, to save the day. The casting in Warlock: The Armageddon, is unintuitive. The main protagonist looks like a bully and we don't buy his romantic story.

The special effects are fine. The gore is particularly well done. More time is spent inside and in the dark than in Part 1, so we end up with a more generically looking horror film. At least, this sequel is scarier, as a result, than its predecessor. Warlock has a new and more interesting assortment of magic spells. You guessed it; contrary to Part 1, this is a slasher flick!

Let's disregard the fact that Warlock just time traveled three centuries ahead and already knows how to drive a car. Let's overlook his stereotypical motivations. Let's also forget that our wizard just turned into the anti-Christ. We're here to have some fun with a combination of horror movie formulas that never fail: gore, witchcraft and a strong body count.

5/8

WWW.TERROR.CA

SOMETIMES THEY COME BACK... AGAIN

1996

A man is mentally tortured by the demonic reincarnations of bullies from his childhood.

Sometimes They Come Back... Again is a remake, more than it is a sequel, to the decent 1991 Sometimes They Come Back, adapted from a short story by Stephen King. In its best moments, this is a basic supernatural slasher. The body count is high, the make-up ambitious, and the effects generally better than the original. The script is well paced and denser.

The cast is composed of familiar faces. The leading antagonist, unlike his sidekicks, is played by a strong, unusual actor that inspires fear through facial gesture and mannerism. Protagonists are given flash backs, a religious procedural and occult hocus-pocus to deal with, converse about, while the good stuff happens elsewhere. Consequently, some subplots feel detached, unnecessary.

While some characters have a dramatic story arc, others are directed to play it slapstick and are treated like slasher cattle. Both moods work fine, but the contrast hurts continuity. This is released in a time of quick cuts and heavy reliance on post-production. Some effects are practical but then some are cheap CG. All in all, this one hits and misses but is more entertaining than the original.

SOMETIMES THEY COME BACK

1991

A history teacher's students reported missing are being replaced by bullies from his past.

Sometimes They Come Back isn't the best short story adaptation to ever come out of a book by Stephen King, but it's not the worst either. This one is rather dialog-driven, but is surreal enough to keep the audience interested. The performances are strong and the bad guys, a bunch of rockabilly, are an interesting cast.

The first act lets us presume the antagonists are ghosts, demons, revenant, or some sort of hybrid. The line is never fully traced and the ambiguity works to the film's advantage. They are basically violent, classic bullies from the 50's but enhanced by immortality. This is the kind of villain that laughs at you and humiliates you before it kills you. Creepy!

Sometimes They Come Back shouldn't constantly bombard us with flashbacks, visions and dream sequences, and shouldn't rely so much on editing. A lot happens in the protagonist's head and it mostly doesn't translate well. A more intricate cinematography could have conveyed his thoughts more clearly, but, as it stands, the movie is simply decent and, sadly, not memorable.

WWW.TERROR.CA

SCANNERS III: THE TAKEOVER

1991

A woman with psychic abilities becomes hungry for power.

Scanners 3 is so simple minded it makes us feel dumb. The two first films were no masterpieces but they were more mature. The studio wasted no time, after the last installment, and came up with this third one; the same year Part 2 was released. Things start with a big "what the hell" moment so dumb and gratuitous we can't look away and can't help but smile.

This is a popcorn movie. It's a visual disaster but an entertaining one; more entertaining than Part 2, that is. The "scanners" are finally elevated to the state of superheroes. They're treated like super mutants. What's more, the psychic gimmick is sporadically being turned into slapstick comedy. What a hilarious mess this movie is, intentionally or not.

Ironically, Scanners 3 is pretty much from the same artists as the previous film. The tone is completely different, though. On top of everything, this flick is a slasher. It is unprecedented, easy on the brain and completely hectic. We get to know the villain more than the hero and it make things exponentially interesting. The creators probably had a blast with this one and we can feel it.

5/8

CASTLE FREAK

1995

A man inherits a castle haunted by a monster.

You'll remember two things from this movie long after the end credits roll: the castle and the freak. Jeffrey Combs does what he does best, that is, get in big trouble, in yet another adaptation of a H.P. Lovecraft short story. Stuart Gordon, director, leverages every inch of this castle. This is an extremely immersive place and it's not a set. It's the real thing.

Castle Freak is more emotionally charged than your average Full Moon Pictures presentation. The chemistry between Jeffrey Combs and Barbara Crampton's characters and their daughter, played by Jessica Dollarhide, is poignant. He's a cheater, she has baggage, the daughter is blind. They all survived a car accident, and nothing has been the same ever since.

People say the castle is "haunted", but that's not exactly it. A hideous thing is trapped there and soon released. It then lurks in the hallways and rapes women, including Combs' daughter and a prostitute he brings home. In a nutshell, this is a cheesy flick with an oversimplified script that is taken very seriously, which gives it a weird dramatic angle.

5/8

MIKEY

1992

A seemingly innocent boy causes death and mayhem in his new neighborhood.

Obviously inspired by 1990's Problem Child, mixed with the tropes of thrillers of the decade, and about as predictable as horror movies with psychotic kids get, Mikey is well-made but barely tolerable. Some scenes are particularly embarrassing, and usually involve Mikey in the presence of boobs. He has the hots for his babysitter and walks in on his naked adoptive mom while she's taking a bath.

Now the strange thing about this movie is we're not exactly sure who it's supposed to entertain. There are enough kids in the plot to attract young audiences, but no parent in their right mind would let their nine-year-old watch this. On the other hand, the film isn't terribly gory, and Mikey isn't the killing machine the promo would like us to believe he is.

Additionally, I can't really imagine a mature adult having a blast, here. The script takes us by the hand and is very robotic. It doesn't even fully indulge in its premise, giving Mikey second thoughts and compassion every now and then. Someone had to make this movie and here it is, as cliché as possibly imaginable. At least Brian Bonsall, who plays Mikey, isn't obnoxious. It helps...

5/8

KILLER TONGUE

1996

A meteorite crashes on Earth, transforming a woman into a mutant with a giant, voracious tongue.

Killer Tongue is a Spanish/English production, and I wouldn't even point it out if it didn't matter. Interestingly, the two biggest actors are imported from the United States. We're talking Melinda Clarke and Robert Englund. In terms of horror, when you think you've seen it all, this is what you should go for. As clumsily directed as it is, there's a crowd for it.

The film has its kinky moments, and yes, some involve Melinda Clarke. I figured there'd be some of that, and it's never as hot as what's crossing your mind right now. This isn't porn! It's gross, actually. It's vulgar. That tongue POV shot never gets sexy. But hey, someone had to make a movie about an evil tongue and writer/director Alberto Sciamma raised his hand.

There are trannies, if that's your thing, there's a bunch of nuns too, and you get Clarke and Englund wearing leather or not much else. The best moments of this film involve Clarke battling her giant tongue and mutilating herself, which is as BDSM as horror gets. If there's one thing you'll remember long after the end credits roll, it's just how much it fucked with your mind.

5/8

DEMONIC TOYS

1992

The blood of a dead policeman resuscitates a demon and its personal toy army inside an overstock warehouse.

This film works for the same reasons 1989's Puppetmaster, also by Full Moon Entertainment, did. The limited cinematography and effects cannot compete with something like Child's Play, though. Although praised by horror fans, evil dolls and toys are a rare thing in horror. They require complex animatronics and puppetry that this film struggles to rig and animate decently.

It is Demonic Toys' innocence that makes it to stand out, charm the viewers and allow them to overlook obvious visual flaws. The story is easy-going, not overly complicated but still dense. The film wants to depict an elaborate mythology despite a low budget, and succeeds against all odds. The musical signature is not just fitting but good. It seems made to scare a child, but then there is gore...

While the dolls and toys make this film an instant classic, it would've been better off without its annoyingly dubbed archvillain. He is the devil, no less, and takes away from the imaginative folklore instigated earlier because he is the only antagonist that isn't a pure creation of the makers. Two characters are played by kids and deliver a painful performance. The rest of the cast is decent.

4/8

SILENT NIGHT, DEADLY NIGHT 5: THE TOY MAKER

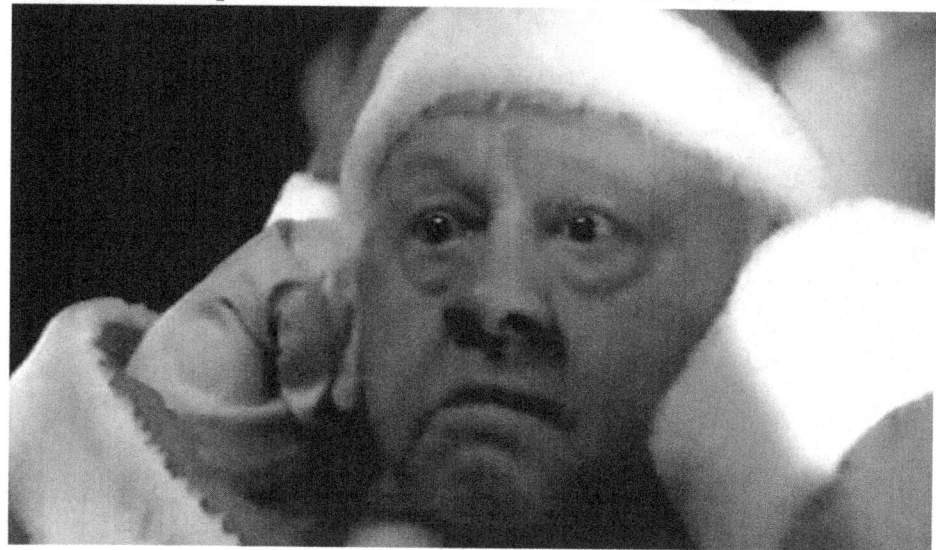

1991

A toy maker and his son design a collection of evil toys to kill kids on Christmas.

This shameless franchise has known more downs than ups. With the inclusion of a still wobbly Part 5, it keeps spiraling downward despite instigating great concepts. Like the last two movies, this one contains strong supernatural elements. In fact, it uses the Christmas gimmick more quintessentially than its predecessor did. Every Holiday cliché is used in a creative way to either scare or kill.

Overall, this is more than a decent slasher. Many clever practical effects are used to animate the possessed toys. They move and kill much like robotic insects would. Contrary to most previous installments, the actors make an otherwise ludicrous story feel plausible, overcoming one of the major ball and chain of the past: overacting.

Photography was a recurring weakness, too. This is the best looking sequel so far. It's creepy, cheesy and fun; simultaneously or sporadically. The main protagonist is a child and his part is handled well. Most performers appear natural enough to carry a good but flawed script. This is the best of the five movies, but it won't generate a cult following. It's not bad enough to mark the audience.

4/8

CANDYMAN: FAREWELL TO THE FLESH

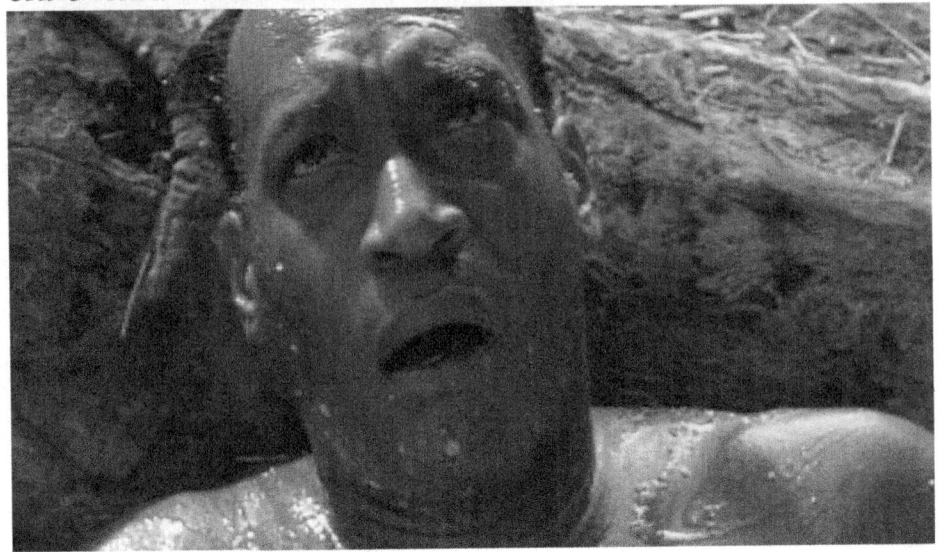

1995

A teacher is visited by a ghost on Mardi Gras.

The tone of this is sequel is similar to that of the original film. The plot includes another procedural school study that leads the protagonist right to Candyman's deadly hook. The formula should work, here, but somehow doesn't. All the winning elements are in place for another success but the director doesn't do much with them. The story in fact hardly ever picks up.

We are moving from the poor neighborhoods of Chicago to New Orleans whose citizens are celebrating Mardi Gras. This drills a hole in the mythos, considering Candyman's ghost should mostly be attached to Cabrini Green, the poor vertical neighborhood that frightened us the first time around. The new setting sucks all the mysticism out of the infamous character.

Candyman's backstory is laid out in front of us, and it somehow conflicts with our preconceptions. This film at least solidifies the villain as a romantic figure that is only evil because he died tragically. The attempts at making us sympathize with him through use of flack backs only cluster the narrative and destroy the mystery. It compromises an already wobbly script.

4/8

DOLLY DEAREST

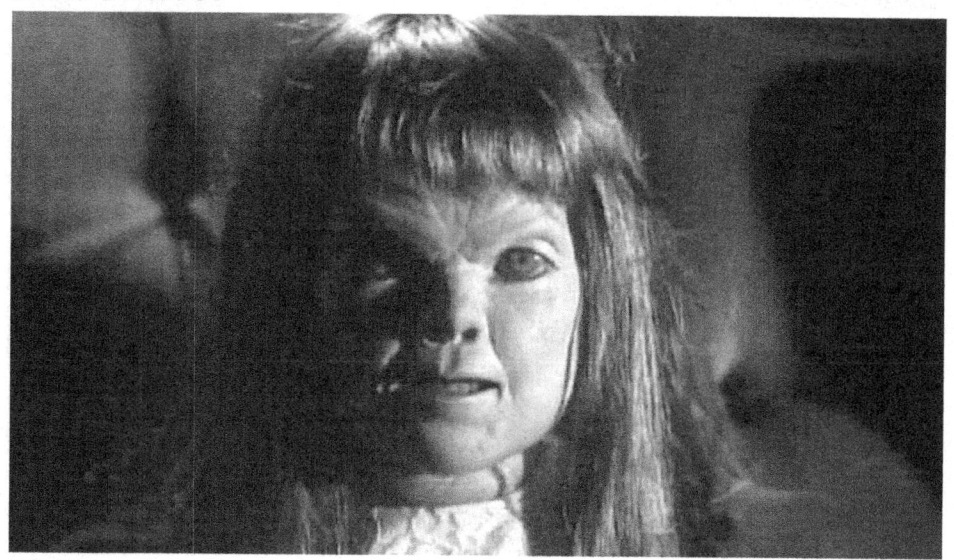

1991

A young girl receives a possessed doll.

By attempting to be everything that Child's Play isn't, Dolly Dearest ends up with the bronze medal of killer doll movies. For instance, there is absolutely no reason why this story should take place in Mexico with American characters other than to stand out and contradict, considering that Chucky was an all-American doll. Also, that whole religious angle is the last thing we need.

The film should embrace its dumb premise. This should be nothing but fun. It isn't rocket science. The child actors aren't particularly likable and can't act. In fact, none of these actors have any kind of appeal; not even Denise Crosby who couldn't care less about this film. The dialogue doesn't work. It's not natural and it doesn't flow. The murders are extremely complicated and weird.

Too much time is spent in that damn cave. If we wanted a movie about archaeology, we'd watch National Geographic. We don't need half the mythos the creators are shoving down our throats. The only good thing about Dolly Dearest is how creepy the doll looks. The puppetry is impressive. This is the stuff of nightmares. These few moments are genuinely frightening but far and few between.

4/8

LEPRECHAUN 2

1994

A leprechaun chases down a woman whose ancestor he once married.

Leprechaun 2 attempts to tie every bit of mythos it can dig up in Irish folklore to a story involving whole new characters. After being greeted with a short anticlimactic retelling of events that took place in medieval times, we're spoon-fed a quick backstory involving slaves and a forced wedding. This sequel takes itself more seriously than the original, doesn't stand out as much, but isn't bad.

Some scenes are shot in a tavern, some in caves seemingly made of plastic, and some in the wild. Leprechaun terrorizes whoever compromises his goal, as usual, but in a St-Patrick's Day context, this time around. It works to the film's advantage but it is underused in the plot and doesn't really spice up the ambiance. The actors do a good job but they're too dramatic for such a ludicrous concept.

It's a well shot movie but it has no visual signature. It does everything a sequel should, but the script is too dense and all over the place. The comedy element greatly suffers from it. 1993's Leprechaun was no masterpiece, but it was marketable and gimmicky enough to generate Leprechaun 2. Because no previous protagonist returns, this new franchise basically relies on a cool slasher monster.

4/8

CANDYMAN: DAY OF THE DEAD

1999

A ghost haunts his distant relative.

From the first scenes, you can already tell that the production value once more dropped a notch. The acting isn't up to par either. There are way too many flashbacks, omens and other cheap plot devices this franchise has been relying on for too long. It weighs on us, the audience, and it's starting to get out of control. Both the performances and the story are becoming hard to sit through.

It does have its moment, though, in how it handles its murder scenes, for instance, but lacks effective build-up and contains no scary scene living up to the original film. At its core, it's a romantic ghost story supported by a procedural. In those terms, it respects its own formula. The problem is that it brings nothing new that the slightly more competent Part 2 didn't already cover.

Perhaps Candyman 3's biggest mistake is to use the previous films as a template while disregarding Clive Barker's intrinsic atmosphere. His movies always kindled unusual emotions, were dense in content, but didn't spell out every answer to their mysteries the way Candyman 3 does. This film is a bad sequel because it can't deal with the mythos, but it is a decent stand-alone film nonetheless.

4/8

976-EVIL II

1992

A sly cursed hotline manipulates a man into performing evil acts.

Quality-wise, this holds up as a sequel. Like the original, character development is not neglected and neither is tension, although the build-up could be handled better. The pacing is unusual and it still works. 976-Evil used to be about an oddly assorted bunch of teens and this time around it goes out of its ways to introduce the concept of astral projection.

It makes three unpardonable continuity mistakes. Firstly, returning character Spike and everyone else, strangers to him, start off troubled or traumatized; all separately exposed to the threat too early. Incidentally, the tone is always dark, always too serious. We lost the signature humor and the wit and it's a shame. Finally, it chooses to humanize an antagonist better left ambiguous.

On the plus side, the sets are atmospheric, well lit and textured. When not inside a 50's diner or an occult store, we're swimming alone in a public pool or sucked inside a television set. Despite its many fault, 976-Evil 2 does some good. Like its predecessor, it becomes increasingly creative as you hit the third act. The cast is older, which means the tone is more mature. We lost teenage perk...

4/8

GHOULIES III: GHOULIES GO TO COLLEGE

1991

Magical creatures released from a cursed comic book are used for vengeance.

The Ghoulies franchise quickly figured out it should be summed up as more than a cheap collection of barely decent practical effects. It did a good job injecting humor and giving its creature a suitable environment in the first sequel and it now transports its monsters inside a surreal college that sets the tone for a caricature of cheesy 80's horror movies.

The pacing is frantic, the camera moves fast and the many shots are short even when they don't need to be. It indicates structure flaws in the script. Sadly, it's nothing the director could fix from his end of the pipeline. You'll find the film lacks a sense of chronology and rhythm. This becomes most evident when we are forced to assist to mysterious sequences of sped up frames.

This is yet another addition in a campy franchise known for its safe and accessible scares. The animatronics are sufficient but we've seen better; the Chucky doll and the gremlins, namely. For this reason, Ghoulies 3 takes the Road Runner path, hoping to stand out, and delivers a slapstick rendition of its past self. Some Ghoulies completists might find this is the best of the three films so far.

4/8

HALLOWEEN: THE CURSE OF MICHAEL MYERS

1995

People once victims of a notorious serial killer unite to break his curse as he returns to his home town.

One of the most depressing sequels to Halloween, and featuring underdeveloped characters that are hard to care for, The Curse of Michael Myers feels the need to complexify and provide backstory about his villain. The movie starts bleakly and remains so until the final scene, so the tension never really drops.

The film is not only dark in tone but in photography as well. The cinematography is more polished than it ever was. The same cannot be said about the script, although it tries hard to tie this with the previous films. Michael Myers's family is at the center of it, for anyone who cared, and returning characters are introduced but recast.

The shots are annoyingly framed. Every shot feels like a close-up. Expect a fine polish, though, a new bad-ass rendition of the Shape, a lot of what you want, but then a lot of what you don't. Be warned that nobody smiles in this. Even the only returning actor, Donald Pleasence, is painfully delivering his lines. That said, he acts as lubricant and as quality stamp in regard to continuity.

4/8

PIRANHA

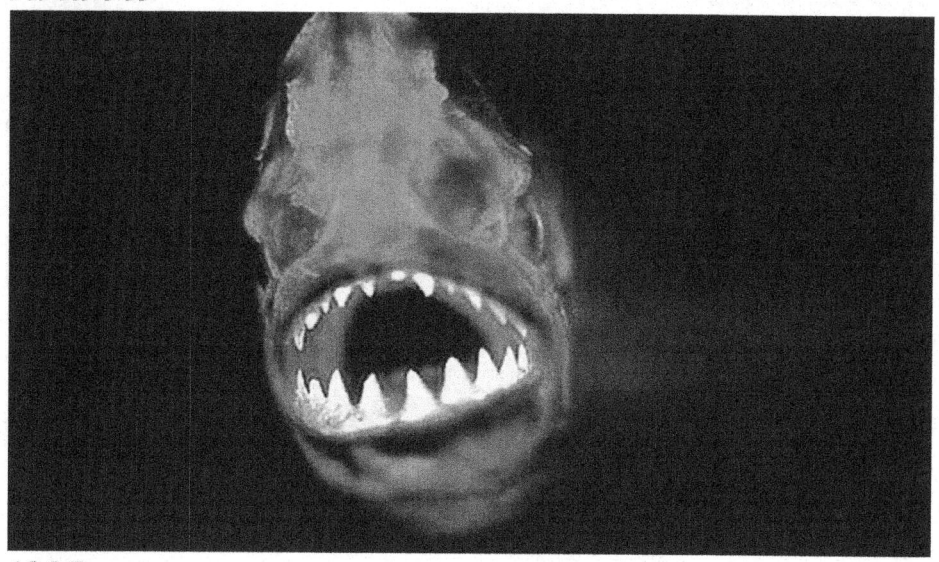

1995

A private investigator discovers that piranhas are killing people.

Who would've though 1978's Piranha needed a remake, and why so soon? This is a film about mutated fishes without much meat on its bone. We still get those shaky underwater visuals when the fishes attack, but the audio effect isn't the same we had in Piranha 1 & 2. Repetition aside, this might as well be part 3. This is a redundant franchise that chases its tail at this point.

It behaves like a TV film but isn't one. It isn't as shocking as its predecessors but still contains decent gore. The photography is rather monotone and its characters aren't energetic. This is the soap opera version of two better films by the same title. It's a movie only hardcore fans of killer fishes could love! It is yet another homage and parody of Jaws that can't live up to the classic.

Some moments of tension work better than others. Build-up isn't Piranha's best feature. Stereotypical characters are also a problem. Cops are particularly clichéd, here. We get a shady business man, an opportunistic film director and the woman who would do anything to play in his productions, including showing skin. Meanwhile, we're not spending our precious time with the piranha...

4/8

WWW.TERROR.CA

THE DENTIST 2

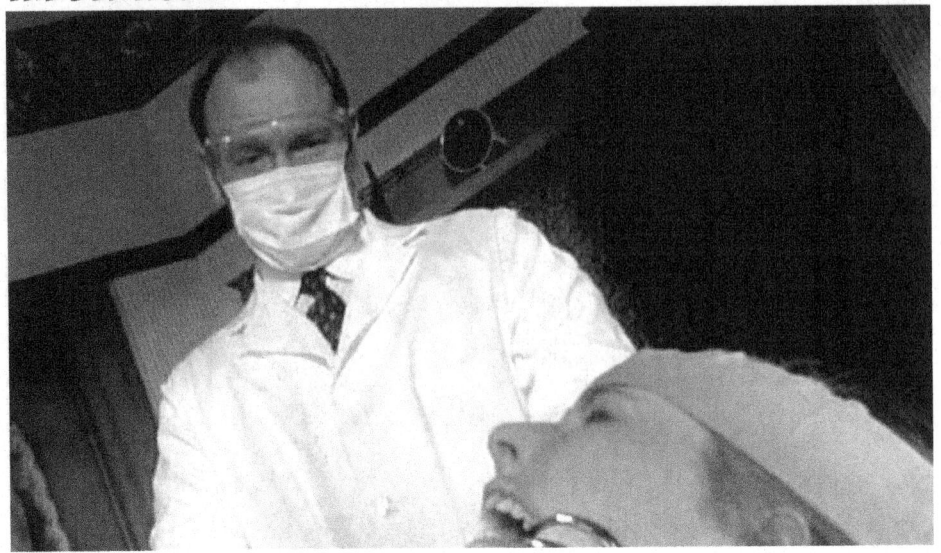

1998

A neurotic dentist moves to a small town and starts killing his new patients.

Effort is invested in making us care and sympathize for the antagonist of the previous film, or at least in providing a backstory. He still suffers hallucinations symbolized by lazy skewing of the picture. The post-production effects are the sequel's greatest flaw. We are witnessing a transition between practical and CG techniques, these days, and it feels cheap in this case.

The dentist's visions aren't so relevant to the plot, but serve the narrative supporting his descent into madness. This said, the compositing techniques match the original signature, making this sequel cohesive and continuous. The first story was pure, quintessential, and introduced us to a mysterious man. This one isn't as memorable, though it mostly meets its own standards.

It's a rural version of what we've already been through. Corbin Bernsen is getting used to his part and is having a blast with it. He plays his part minimally, keeps his crazy face for the right moments and it pays off. The movie is a simple one and doesn't cover much ground, but contains a good amount of chills and gore. It's a silly concept if you overthink it, but it's entertaining otherwise.

4/8

SLUMBER PARTY MASSACRE III

1990

Teenagers die by the hand of a masked mass murderer during a slumber party.

Slumber Party Massacre 3 is a return to sources. Part 2 had turned its villain into a dream spirit and brought strong supernatural elements where there were none, but this one behaves like a plausible teen slasher with no allusion to the previous film. What matters is that we have a drill-wielding murderer terrorizing bubbly girls for who slumber party rhymes with full frontal nudity.

This amount of character exposition is so ludicrous, considering the superficial plot, that we can't resist being seduced by the cohesive cast. The do not even have the luxury of a stereotype to impersonate; they feel like one and the same and it still works. Slumber Party Massacre 3's weaknesses are also its charms: the dialog is empty and infantilizing when not fascinatingly uncomfortable.

Girls dance and strip for each other. The guys then join them, soon followed by the pizza guy and a psychopath that uses common tropes of horror, including plenty of gore, to turn this sequel into something worth watching for the fan. It is better filmed and edited than the previous entries and not as surreal. It plays by the numbers for a while and gets interesting in the second half.

4/8

SORORITY HOUSE MASSACRE II

1990

A sisterhood is targeted by a serial killer.

Early on, we see footage from 1982's The Slumber Party Massacre and its serial killer, old Hokstedter, dispatching most of a cast in a few seconds. The murderer in Sorority House Massacre Part 1 was a completely different character, which brings a great deal of confusion from the get go. We're then introduced, in real time, to yet another stalking creep that may or may not be our next psycho.

This is followed by a marathon of five gratuitous boob shots; two in the shower, two in a bedroom and one in the living room. A Ouija board séance featuring the sisters in undies drinking alcohol follows. This is to be expected from a horror movie with the word sorority in its title and is something to experience. The bad dialog, timing and editing makes this more cliched than it has to be.

This is a fun film to watch. It is simple-minded, has a limited cast and set and a very simple story. It makes two unforgivable mistakes. First, it alludes to a supernatural element that it barely exploits; second, it puts too much emphasis on a police procedural that hardly ties in with the main plot, especially when considering that the current killer may originate from a different franchise.

4/8

THE UNNAMABLE II: THE STATEMENT OF RANDOLPH CARTER

1992

A strange creature haunts a university.

If you cope with this odd film, it will make you giggle sporadically and you'll have a good time. The monster was scary in Part 1 but is fully exposed now and lost its effect. The love interest stays naked much longer than she needs to, up until someone concludes "there should be clothes on her". This is a cheesy horror flick inspired by the works of H.P. Lovecraft and it is more fun than scary.

The new plotline is obscure and will make the Lovecraft fans geek out. We go further, this time around, in the Cthulhu mythos and deeper underground, too. Everything is more extreme, but everything is more spood-fed as well. The new cast is interesting. David Warner and John Rhys-Davies make this film somewhat more compelling than The Unnamable Part 1, though it is not a better movie as a whole.

The editing is a little rough around the edges. Scene transitions are abrupt. Also, whatever worked in the first act gets tired in the second one only to pick up again in the last act. The character of Alyda is annoying and, as it turns out, she is the center of the story. She brings this movie down and is poorly performed. Once again, the score is cheap and often inappropriate.

4/8

MANIAC COP 2

1990

A revenant who used to be a cop is after the people who killed him while he was in prison.

Bruce Campbell delivers a good but last performance as the returning protagonist before meeting his end by the hands of what we assume to be the original revenant cop. A new lead, Robert Davi, makes this feel once more like a detective story by approaching its villain as a complete stranger, allowing this movie to revisit its original idea at a convenient slow pace.

The villain is well fleshed out now. He has style, he's got moves. Using his cap as a mask to cover his face, he is a true horror icon, at this point, and the production is putting him on a pedestal, as he deserves. The photography and the editing, and the whole production value, were upped a notch.

The curious mix of police action and slasher horror is once again presented here. We get another long chase sequence that's right out of a car chase flick. Everything is a little bit better in this sequel except for the hardly plausible plot device involving an improbable serial killer that the maniac cop befriends. It complicates the story and degrades our antagonist.

4/8

TREMORS II: AFTERSHOCKS

1996

A Mexico town is invaded by morphing creatures.

This so-so sequel brings back some of its actors and characters, but Kevin Bacon is nowhere to be found. He had a presence that returning performers Fred Ward and Burt Gummer can't match. The original film relied on mystery and suspense, something Part 2 can't afford because we've seen the beasts and know what they do. This said, the writers aren't short of ideas to spice up the mythology.

The framework of rules established by Part 1 is not only followed and honored but stacked on top of a new one. For one thing, Mexican Graboids are revealed to be morphing creatures. The new monster designs; both CG and practical, are not as creepy and mysterious as they have been and should remain. The new monsters are nowhere as interesting as the previous ones and the gimmick suffers from it.

Tremors 2 is as good as direct-to-video sequels get and is worth a watch, though fans of Part 1 shouldn't set their expectations high. Unfortunately, with its best cards already played, the film resorts to cheaper comedy, plays it cool and simple-minded. The vast desert backdrop is the best character, here, and compensates for flaky video compositing, bad dialog and a sad lack of signature.

4/8

JACK FROST

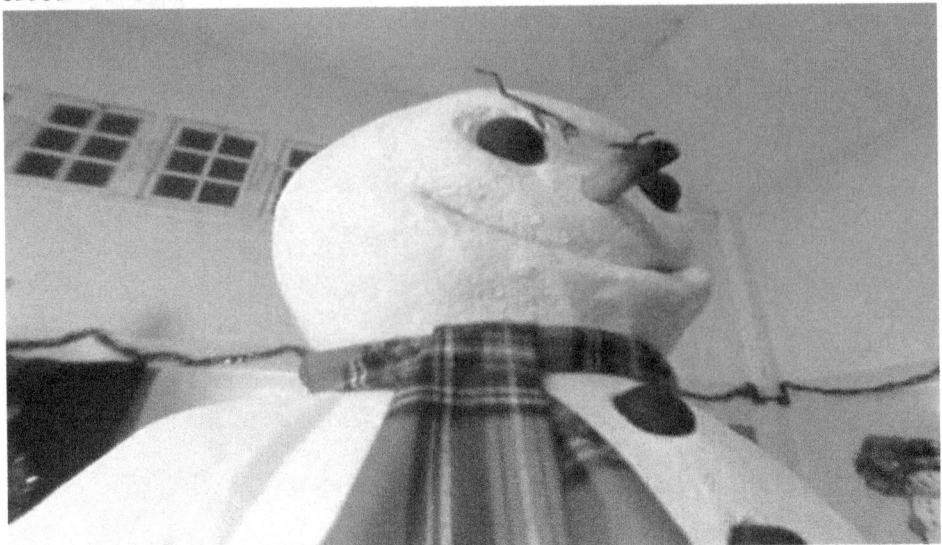

1997

A dead criminal reincarnates as a snowman and terrorizes a suburban neighborhood.

This is the badly edited and clumsily post processed story of a dying murderer possessing a snowman. It's as bad as it sounds, but it's going straight for laughs, which it doesn't always get. The limited budget doesn't allow a production as cohesive and enjoyable as the Child's Play movies are. The plot is similar but the gimmick only wants to cash-in on the holiday spirit and a winning formula.

It's cute if you want a Christmas themed horror movie, but there's better out there. The photography is poor by most standards. The dialog isn't much better. The various practical effects are basic and nothing we haven't seen a hundred times before. Of course, you get gore, one-liners and other immature jokes, but nothing worth the franchise the makers obviously wish they could generate.

The funniest parts of Jack Frost involve decent actors pretending to care, and care way too much, about trivial details pertaining to the supernatural villain's singularities. Not much makes sense in the plot and fighting an evil snowman with logic reasoning and strategy is so ludicrous it can't be done with a straight face. It is why the film is worth watching once despite how terrible it is.

4/8

OMEN IV: THE AWAKENING

1991

A young girl with demonic powers kills those who oppose her.

The original Antichrist was a young boy who killed people using the power of his mind and with the implicit help of the devil. We followed his story in a way that sometimes made him a protagonist and made us understand how he would grow to gain political influence by the third film. This remake goes nowhere this interesting and meets none of the previous standards.

This franchise used to reach levels of quality found nowhere here. Depictions of death and catastrophes are underdone and the stakes appear lower. This is a TV movie with cheap photography that sets the wrong tone. It doesn't dare fully assume the gore and scares required by the gimmick. It should be a mature movie with a fun gimmick but it can't handle subtlety.

Damien used to be creepy and "Delia" is angry. By trying to re-invent the wheel, the makers end up turning in circles with a cliched fusion between the original Omen and Carry. They offer nothing new. It's not grandiose, it's not visually nourishing and it relies on a magical element it can't juggle with. Sadly, this barely decent supernatural thriller is melodramatic and neglects suspense.

4/8

PSYCHO COP RETURNS

1993

An evil cop kills people partying inside an office building.

In the first movie, the action took place around a pool, in a car and in the woods. This time, the possessed cop goes after rebels throwing a secret party with prostitutes in their office. The antagonist's aversion to crime is reinforced, along with his persona. This is a moral trope popularized by the Friday the 13th franchise. The script fools no one here: the sinners get slashed...

The picture is cleaner; photography is more compelling and the still amateur editing is at least tighter. Although the acting is bad, any performance in this tops the previous ones. Flirting, nudity and sexuality are at the center of protagonist exposition and the movie is still unnecessarily awkward about it all. Despite some innovation, Pycho Cop Returns is nothing more than the copy of a copy.

This film struggles but generally tries harder. Robert R. Shafer returns as the villain and updates his delivery according to the adjustments made to his character. His temper's been calmed and it makes the movie more tolerable. He blends in more easily and doesn't desperately beg to join the high ranks of famous horror icon anymore. He steers away from the generic presence he had in Part 1 a bit.

4/8

OFFICE KILLER

1997

A mousy office worker accidentally kills one of her coworkers, then proceeds to bump off a few others.

Scream and Scream 2, 1996 and 1997 respectively, bitch slapped this film into Oblivion, and every other slasher that came out around that time for that matter. From then on, filmmakers could no longer be lazy. Films with hooks this lame would never get greenlit, at least not for a few years. Thirty minutes in, I still couldn't figure out what Office Killer was about.

I just didn't give a damn about the characters. You get a lot of hamming from almost all performers, perhaps to compensate for how bland the film looks. From the dull production design to the sluggish lighting, there's something off about the ambiance. From what I could tell, around halfway in, this was a sitcom with accidental deaths in it. And, for a comedy, it's really not that funny.

Every time I screamed "Eureka!"; every aha moment I had, led to yet another ten minutes of dialogue. I just didn't get this film. It rubbed me the wrong way. The quality was there, the actors were good, but this story went nowhere. Its ultimate demise was to glorify strangeness over clarity. And, by the way, a film like this one shouldn't need four writers.

4/8

FUNNY MAN

1994

After winning a stately house in a game of poker, a record producer finds it to be haunted by a demonic jester.

If there's one thing we learned from 1990's horror movies, it's that your expectations don't matter. People wanted novelty. Simon Sprackling will surprise you at every turn, with style and no substance. Funny Man isn't your typical slasher film. It's British, for one thing, and it breaks the fourth wall every chance it gets. The score is right out of a circus, even when people are being killed.

You know, that 1980's horror film with a scary jester offing protagonists one by one after they've had premarital sex? Well, this isn't that movie. We're way passed that. The world ends in 6 years, people. We need to revolutionize the genre! This is what the 90's fisheye lens is for. This is the reason half the characters are right out of Mad Max. It's the reason this film is so atrocious.

Funny Man throws weird stuff your way every two minutes, like that Velma look-alike, who turns this investigation into a Scooby Doo episode for a while. It's hard to keep up with. It's a complicated movie. Films like these are the reason people say 90's horror sucked. It's disjointed. It seems to have been made by someone who hates horror movies. That jester is creepy, though...

CRITTERS 3

1991

An apartment building is invaded by small alien creatures.

The significant drop in effort and quality deeply hurts this sequel. The actors don't seem cued properly and the writers can't keep up with the increasingly delightful eccentricities of the first two films. Probably declared TKO during pre-production, this one gets lazy with puppetry. The directing is dowdy. Most of the characters aren't returning and the ones we are given aren't likable.

The city setting doesn't come much into play. The plot takes place in a building depicted as a fortress for the crites to conquer, which probably sounds more entertaining than it is. We mostly follow kids, making this addition in the series as accessible as the previous installments were if not more. Don Keith Opper and Terrence Mann interpret their mastered critter parts again.

The trademark science-fiction cheese is absent, the suspense is ineffective and the crites aren't funny, which leaves us with very little to feast on. Critters 3 takes every shortcut it meets and chooses minimalism over depth, therefore reducing a ludicrous concept to now legitimate preconceptions the general moviegoer has of the franchise. The film's not bad, but it's dumber than it should be.

3/8

HARD TO DIE

1990

In a skyscraper, employees of a lingerie company are terrorized by a murderer.

Hard to Die is a movie about women who like taking showers who run into trouble the day they receive a mysterious package. Every excuse is good for frontal nudity. The girls work overtime in a lingerie company and enjoy trying on samples. This film uses Sorority House Massacre 2 as a plot template and subtracts the sisterhood. Some actors return in comparable roles; some wear the same clothes.

The action takes place in a skyscraper instead of a sorority house. To make continuity even more chaotic, scenes from The Slumber Party Massacre are rehashed and retold by the janitor to scare the female characters the same way they were warned in Sorority House Massacre 2. The acting is terrible, the framing and photography just as bad, but somehow the movie is highly entertaining.

It is conceivable that the makers underestimated how funny the film they were making would end up being. The writers go from A to B but make a detour through Z to tell a very simple story. Hard to Die is so bad it is good. It cares about showing skin more than it cares about continuity, effects, editing and pacing. It is impossible to watch with a straight face. It is hilariously imperfect.

PROM NIGHT IV: DELIVER US FROM EVIL

1992

An obsessed religious fanatic hunts down teenagers to punish them for their sins.

The original Prom Night was as simple as slashers get and was followed by two memorable supernatural movies. The villain is a dangerous serial killing cleric who reveals his identity early on and therefore doesn't come with red herrings. Stand-alone sequel, Prom Night 4 attempts to propel the franchise in a new direction but with a gimmick much weaker than that any of the previous entries.

Its filmed right, well-written, can be considered a quintessential slasher, but is emotionally distant, rushed and too bleak for its own good. It is one of the rare teen slasher flicks not to use humor to lubricate the audience. It is not aimed at an audience the age of its protagonists, ironically. Despite the plausible subgenre it exploits, it is slow-paced and contains hints of demonology.

If you hate religious subplots, this might still work for you. The killer's M.O. doesn't imply that God and the Devil exist. The only demons here are inside the priest's head, but the tone of the film would have us believe he is supported by a deity. The film feels unique, somewhat fresh, but contains too much filler and isn't exciting enough to keep us passionate until the end.

3/8

CRITTERS 4

1992

The last remaining eggs of an endangered alien species wreak havoc aboard a spaceship.

Critters 4 is not just about "crites" in space, but also in time. It takes place in the future and over a metallic backdrop. Part 3 was too generic and failed, so Part 4 goes all out. Outer space is not such a stretch for a species that came from there, but the audience still has to buy it. Contrary to all previous films, most of the characters are adults. They're also cold and darken the mood.

The animatronics are horrendous and the sets are cheap. The crites get little screen time despite being the only reason we're sitting through odd filler. The franchise were never big on set, costume and production design when it came to alien machinery, mechanisms and physics, but this is a new low. We're in the future, people dress the way we do and computers seem prehistoric...

The best thing this sequel does is dig up the still dormant science-fiction plot devices all movies have used to introduce their creature. The original writers had horror and comedy in mind and didn't get around to exploiting the potential for scientific mythology and backstory. This said, without quirky humor and rigor in the storytelling, we barely scratch the surface.

3/8

LEPRECHAUN 4: IN SPACE

1996

Soldiers attempt to exterminate a Leprechaun in space.

Critters and Aliens can go to space when the producers run out of gimmicks because it is pertinent to their respective premise. They both dealt with a species from outer space and the Irish leprechaun isn't one. There was always an element of comedy in the Leprechaun movies, but they were based off a supernatural slasher template. This film instead resorts to cheap humor and science-fiction.

Fans of the three first films will hate on it. The dialog is uneasy, it is poorly written, directed, and actors reek of TV series science-fiction. The movie uses a light saber and other popular references as important plot elements and adopts a narrative similar to 1986's Aliens. There is very little the writer came up with himself, and not all effects look as good as he presumably imagined.

Warwick Davis is having a blast using guns and dodging grenades. This is the inevitable moment in a franchise where the antagonist meets a serious arsenal. Slasher icons need to be immortal for their respective franchises to be as well. Leprechaun 4 makes two crucial and obvious mistakes: it takes place in space for no relevant reason and it brings the army in; sucking all the horror out...

CHILDREN OF THE CORN V: FIELDS OF TERROR

1998

After their car broke down, a group of college students find themselves stuck in a town overtaken by a cult.

Some of the previous films in the series could be described as supernatural slashers. This formula works as long as the effects aren't terrible. This is an issue, here. The protagonists look like they're in their early twenties and the premise of car trouble is cliché territory. Another problem surfaces when we encounter our first brute; a "kid" who looks way too old to be called that.

None of the younger actors are doing a good job, sadly. No aspect of the film is better than decent; an ongoing annoyance in the Children of the Corn franchise. Kids can be made creepy under the right lens, but for the 5th time they aren't. This sequel neither reinvents itself, nor does it offer a creative take on the original material. It is too busy accumulating plot holes as it goes.

This is one of the best looking one so far, yet it has the polish and melodrama of a TV movie. It only appears like a better product because it makes use of digital footage rather than photographic film. Short on corn, on children and shy on gore, aside from a certain artistic quality, it has little to offer to back its title and contains too few story arcs we haven't already covered.

3/8

SILENT PREDATORS

1999

A small town deals with a rattlesnake invasion.

Humans are greedy. Humans destroy natural habitat. Snakes get angry. Snakes kill. This made-for-TV film is halfway between a soap opera with snakes and a typical, actually angry snake movie. It's kind of dumb, but it contains none of the tongue-in-cheek humor you'd expect. You're never sure if you should take this film seriously. Well, in the end, it's rather serious... way too serious.

The post-production editing can get annoying. Fortunately, the snakes aren't in 3-D. They don't appear to be stock footage either, but they don't directly interact with the actors. The illusion is charming, but if you think about what you are watching, you'll see that the snakes are framed separately. This probably required strong synchronism, but it doesn't fool anyone.

No horror movie about a snake invasion goes without its environmental commentary. Silent Predators is no exception. Politicizing the antagonist has always been a thing in these films, and it's a device that pretty much writes itself. Sadly, this film has been made many times before and much better. John Carpenter contributed to the teleplay but we don't feel his magic touch.

3/8

NIGHT OF THE DRIBBLER

1990

A weak college basketball team lose their best players one by one at the hands of a mysterious killer.

Night of the Dribbler looks and feels like a Troma Entertainment film, and if this sounds like a good thing, by all means stop whatever you're doing and put this on. Everyone else, brace yourselves. The movie drags and its pacing is atrocious. There's no way to take any of it seriously, and I hope there's a tight cut out there. Had it been sixty minutes long, this could have been exciting.

The script feels like it was written by a seven-year-old. Basketball isn't just the context; it is the core element. In fact, this is a movie about basketball that just happens to have murders in it. The joke gets old. Well into the second half, a question remains: what's the point? It's like the crew got to shoot for two days in a gymnasium and forgot someone might actually watch this crap.

It's a feel-good slapstick horror comedy so bad it's... decent. While no one seems to care that a killer is roaming about, an ongoing detective procedural spoon-feeds us useless details. Just lay back, observe, and have a drink. This is a stupid film, but it grows on you. At some point, you forget you're watching a slasher and you kind of stick around for the cheese.

3/8

STEPFATHER III

1992

A serial killer preying on single mothers infiltrates a new family.

Terry O'Quinn doesn't return and the script wipes the problem off by having the stepfather, Jerry, get plastic surgery. Quality took an irrecoverable drop. The direction is minimalist, the camera is rarely doing what it should and the acting is not convincing. Few thrillers generate franchises like horror movies do because continuity is usually ensured by re-hiring the actor playing the villain.

It goes as far as using humor to mask cheap gore, inviting us to overlook obvious mistakes. The protagonist is a child who sees through the stepfather's subterfuge and looks him up using old implausible computer technology that can be blamed on poor production design. The script is thin and not balanced to feel like the previous two movies. It's too melodramatic and too predictable.

At this point, the stepfather's M.O. begs for creativity. Interchanging the ages and genders of the various kids he terrorized over the years doesn't justify a legacy this size. Every attempt at revamping the franchise feels unpolished; on paper and visually. Good enough for cable TV only, Stepfather 3 lacks energy, musical queues and a decent ambiance. It's watchable but doesn't try hard enough.

3/8

BAD CHANNELS

1992

A radio station is taken over by a robot and an alien.

Bad Channels creates a concept bigger than its budget can allow, and then makes it happen the best it can. The characters are eccentric and are a good diversion from all that is flaky. The sets are limited in size and fabric quality, but are believable enough to get the story across. The comedic tone isn't even, so better hang on to the keen surrealism and the deliberate cheese.

For an alien invasion flick, the stakes aren't very high. It's not a gory film, either. The makers are having fun thinking outside the box for better or worse and in full creativity. The monster rigs are limited so they in fact barely move. Their extra-terrestrial essence is put to use when Bad Channels unexpectedly turns into a musical... and a bad one!

The idea of a haunted broadcast has exploitative potential, but can easily be ruined by an asynchronous score, weak character depiction and superficial editing. There simply isn't suspense or build-up. The characters do have an arc, but their emotional state toggles constantly and, as a result, we don't care about their trouble any more than they themselves do.

CURSE OF THE PUPPET MASTER

1998

A teenager in love is hired as assistant to an eccentric doctor able to inject life into puppets.

In-between puzzling symbolic dream sequences and inapt inserts, we slowly learn to enjoy our three protagonists bathing in a nice Gothic country set. It's the perfect setting for a new start after "The Final Chapter". It's a good thing the leads are so sympathetic because their exposition keeps us from looking too much at the puppets and noticing their poor carving and their cheap rig.

The puppets once looked better, indeed. It seems the makers were hoping to get away with negligence, seeing as footage from the previous films was slipped in during most scenes of interaction between humans and puppets. Even the key moments let us down because the effort isn't there. The budget and the manpower were obviously cut down and it's disconcertingly noticeable.

The various subplots work better on a human level than they ever did. We are finally dealing with somewhat normal individuals, but no investment was made towards quality puppets or puppeteers in this stitched-up horror movie about evil toys that are unfortunately barely animated. The new footage is appreciable but the rehash is unforgivable and certainly not edited in a seamless fashion.

TROLL 2

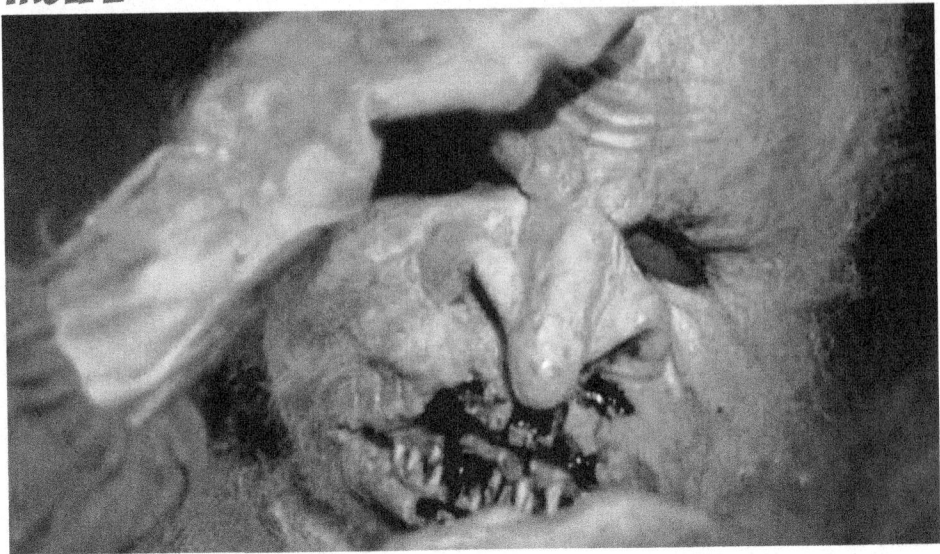

1990

A family moves to a new town unbeknownst to them the kingdom of goblins.

Troll 2 has the signature of a horror film that wants to scare children. Blood is replaced by a green herbal substance that wouldn't be half as creepy if it was red. The main protagonist is a boy who nobody believes when the goo hits the fan, and he appears more scared than most final girls of popular horror features. He should be. This film is a schizophrenic's nightmare...

This is a sequel by name only. We understand this from the first frames in, as a hoard of goblins; dwarves in cheap costumes and certainly not trolls, run around in the woods, sweeping away any hope for franchise continuity. The illusions featured here are not the peculiar practical effects that made Troll memorable. Troll 2 marks the mind for other reasons.

It is politically incorrect, irreverent. It is made in a rush and looks cheap. There appears to have been no chemistry or communication between the creators and the actors. The script has solid ideas that the director renders with terrifying visuals, but the character blocking is mostly missing and, as a result, the performers seem constrained by their unnatural dialog lines and their movements.

TERROR FIRMER

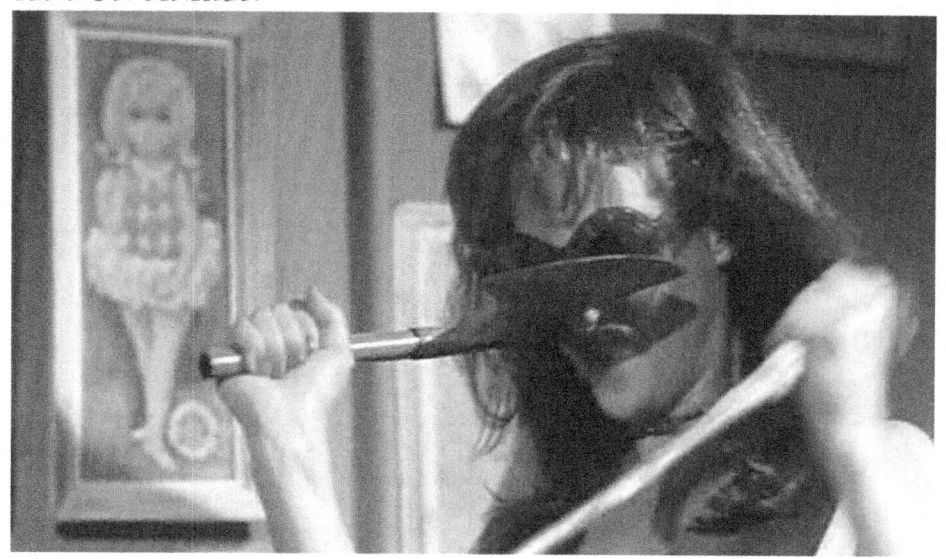

1999

A low-budget film crew must stop a homicidal maniac on the loose.

It's no secret: the Troma family is a strange but welcoming one, where people of all races, sexual identities and orientations gather to make questionable low budget horror comedies. People with disabilities and from various social classes that would otherwise be incompatible unite to create gorefests. In Terror Firmer, toilet jokes, sex jokes, jokes on gays and on pregnancy are abundant.

Terror Firmer is Troma's self-referential feature film. It takes place on the set of what seem like another installment in the Toxic Avenger franchise. But it's also a slasher flick with a female killer. That's different. It contains graphic scenes of softcore porn. Obnoxious applaud noises and various other sounds were added in post-production, in case we didn't realize this was a comedy.

In fact, most of this film is a cacophony. It's out of control. It takes so many detours that we forget what the main plotline is about. Lloyd Kaufman and his creative team aren't perfectionists. Their character blocking, dialogue, costumes, special effects and editing appear half improvised. No matter how sexy this film gets, most of it is so disgusting that we're never turned on.

FOR MORE HORROR-THEMED BOOKS, VISIT WWW.TERROR.CA

Made in the USA
Coppell, TX
06 February 2020

15480887R00066